2/95

D0466730

Always Stand In
Against the Curve

Books by Willie Morris

North Toward Home
Yazoo
Good Old Boy
The Last of the Southern Girls
A Southern Album (with Irwin Glusker)
James Jones: A Friendship
Terrains of the Heart and Other Essays on Home
The Courting of Marcus Dupree
Always Stand in Against the Curve

ALWAYS STAND IN AGAINST THE CURVE

And Other Sports Stories

by

Willie Morris

YOKNAPATAWPHA PRESS

Oxford, Mississippi

Published by Yoknapatawpha Press, Inc.
P.O. Box 248, Oxford, Mississippi 38655

Two of the essays in this book have previously appeared in somewhat different form: "The Phantom of Yazoo" in *The New Yorker* (and later in the book, *North Toward Home,* Houghton Mifflin, 1967); "The Search for Billy Goat Hill" in *Ole Miss Magazine,* 1981.

ISBN 0-916242-25-0   LC 83-50003

Printed in the United States of America
Book design by Lawrence Wells

Contents

Foreword

As I grow older, more often than not I think of myself, in body and in spirit, as I was on a summer's afternoon when I was seventeen years old. This is no mundane confession, and I rather suspect there are others, grown men and women, who also see themselves through old time's prism when they were more or less that age. Surely there is a wisp of immortality in us then, poised at that juncture before the world seizes hold of us. And for many of us, especially from what was the small-town South, sports was a nexus for much that was meaningful to us: dexterity, fulfillment, radiant well-being—and pain and struggle and disappointment.

Indeed, as a writer I have often viewed sports as a metaphor for much that transpired in the greater society, for the shadow beneath the act—a reflection of the American hyperboles. Pondering one sport in particular, Marino Casem, the venerable coach at Alcorn State University in Mississippi, once observed: "In the East college football is a cultural exercise. On the West Coast it is a tourist attraction. In the Midwest it is cannibalism. But in the South it is religion, and Saturday is the holy day."

In the fall of 1981, as I was following the great Marcus Dupree in his senior year in high school for the purposes of a book, my experiences with the Philadelphia High Tornadoes were a vivid conjuring of my own past for me. The poor little playing fields of east central Mississippi, the pale stadium lights swarming with the autumn insects, the ancient yellow school buses, the cheerleaders and baton-twirlers and off-key fight songs, the faithful parents and teachers and pool hall characters brought back for me in an immense rush the fields and diamonds and courts of my own adolescence. Except for the presence of blacks on the playing fields and in the grandstands, not much seemed really to have changed, and I began writing some stories that were enmeshed there in my memory.

I had carried my interest in sports into adulthood, and I am glad I did, for this had linked me over the years in my American comings and goings with a number of good friends in the sporting cosmos: Michael Burke, Jack Whitaker, Lindsey Nelson, Howard

Cosell, Jim Lampley, Bill Bradley, Pete Dawkins, James Dickey, George Plimpton, Dan Jenkins, Bud Shrake, as well as the Mississippians Warner Alford, Dog Brewer, Jake Gibbs, Squirrel Griffing, Bill McCammon, Cobb Jarvis, and others. And life would have been much less tolerable without the countless late-at-night talks and New York sports excursions with Irwin Shaw—"the Old Lion"—whose experiences at Ebbets Field as quarterback of the Brooklyn College Kingsmen in the late 1920s circuitously led him to pen the greatest sports story of them all, "The Eighty-Yard Run."

My comrade Larry L. King of the intractable steppelands of West Texas was also suffused in the rigors and grandeur of sport long before he made a million or two with his *The Best Little Whorehouse in Texas*. Larry was an all-state lineman for Midland High who subsequently performed for the Red Raiders of Texas Tech. Many years later he won a Nieman Fellowship to Harvard. Since he had never received his college degree, he decided to try out for the Harvard football team. He telephoned the athletic department and got an assistant coach on the line, introducing himself as a football player who had just received an academic scholarship to Harvard.

"Fine, Larry," the assistant coach said. "I just need a little information. Did you play in high school?"

"Yessir. I was all-state in Texas."

"At what position?"

"Tackle."

"Have you ever played in college?"

"I played a little for Texas Tech, but I didn't like the academic climate there."

The coach was quite interested now. "How big are you, Larry?"

"I'm six feet and weigh 230 pounds."

"That sounds good. We report for practice Thursday afternoon."

"I'll be there."

"One more thing," the coach said. "How old are you?"

"Forty-one."

"I beg your pardon?"

"I'm 41."

There was a long pause. "Say, what *is* this?" the coach finally asked.

I understood very well what it was, and I hope this little book will help the reader to understand, too.

I want to thank my friends Larry and Dean Faulkner Wells of the irrepressible Yoknapatawpha Press, located over the Sneed Ace Hardware Store on the courthouse square in Oxford, Mississippi, for wanting me to do this book. I am also indebted to Dean's 16-year-old son, the Jaybird, whose photograph adorns the cover. The Jaybird, a consummate athlete, was always a fount of *deja vus* for me, providing resonant echoes in my memory. One recent late afternoon he was travelling with his baseball team to the remote rural hamlet of Thaxton to play the locals. He had never played against tough boondocks boys under such pale lights on a diamond surrounded by cotton and soybeans. We asked if we might buy him a miner's hat. We waited up for him that night, as we often do when he is on the road, and dolefully heard his description of an egregious defeat.

I have taken the liberty of dedicating each of these stories to various people I cherish, sometimes five or six of them at a time. One could not get away with that in New York, but I do not apologize for this most unprofessional yet heartfelt gesture. Had we both world enough and time to tell our friends what they mean to us.

So, in truth, this book is a family album of sorts, something I hope one might come across on a rainy day of the equinox in a hallowed old attic in a settled old town. The section of photographs is meant to complement, not illustrate, the stories. I am grateful to my Yazoo City friends—Norman Mott, Stanley C. Beers, and Kay King Ketchum—for locating many of these photos of old Yazoo, and to Del Litle of W.A. Krueger Company, a baseball man from East Tennessee, for co-ordinating the printing for Yoknapatawpha Press.

I am happy the beloved dog of my childhood, Old Skip, has at last made a photographic appearance. I could not have grown up without Skip, just as I could not have reached middle age without my honored Pete. I know Skip and Pete are friends in dogs' heaven. I can see them now, dallying in a comfortable shade, bereft of ticks and fleas, eating fried chicken livers and rib-eye steak, and thinking—I pray—of the boy-athlete they had to leave.

W.M.
Summer, '83

The Fumble

To Larry L. King

WHEN WE were in the seventh grade, School Superintendent Loren P. Ledbetter did something unbelievable. He put Central High of Jackson on our football schedule for a game five years in the future, compounding the blasphemy by agreeing to play in Jackson. Old Man Ledbetter was strange anyway, and left school three years after that with a vague shadow on his name, but the damage had been done. I remember the afternoon everyone heard what he had gotten us into. "He's lost his marbles," Mr. Chris Wesley told a group of merchants while cutting my hair. "He's crazy as a swamp bird." They all shook their heads. "Jackson Central!"

We were a town of 7,000, half of them colored, sixty miles north of Jackson, a poor little town of undistinguished facades perched there on the banks of our murky river, while Jackson was the capital of Mississippi. It was a brisk metropolis of well over 100,000 citizens with swimming pools and country clubs and mansions with pickaninny statues on the lush lawns and hotels twenty stories high with nightclubs on top which let people bring their own whiskey, and everything touched a little with the Yankee dollar. "The Crossroads of the South," its signs proclaimed. Our families drove all the way to Jackson to shop in Kennington's or The Emporium on Capitol Street, or to take us to the zoo. Central High was the only white high school in the whole city. Its majestic school buildings were right around the corner from the Capitol and the Governor's Mansion and covered an entire block, self-assured and expansive as any university. We knew all about the Central High Tigers as far back as grammar school. They had seventy-five boys or more on their football team and once won thirty-two games in a row, playing in the fabulous Big Eight Conference. Their best players went on to Ole Miss, where they joined SAE or KA and got the reigning delta beauties, then moved successfully into brokerage or real estate, usually in Memphis or Atlanta. Our school, given its size, could barely get thirty boys together and played in the lowly Delta Valley Conference against other little towns out in the flat cotton country.

Shortly after the word got out, Billy Bonner and I were walking down the street toward his house, avoiding the cracks in the sidewalk as was our habit.

"They scheduled us for a *breather*," Billy said suddenly, for Mr. Ledbetter's folly had been worrying him all afternoon. Billy's father, who was the Chevrolet dealer, had once taken us to a game in Jackson. Fifteen thousand people came to those games in the fancy stadium off State Street! And not only from Jackson but from all over middle Mississippi, just to watch the unfolding of the invincible.

Billy paused a moment, then added as if in revelation: "That game's in five years, right? We'll be seniors."

I recall the exact moment Billy said that, because it was a dark, gloomy day of intermittent rain, and a clap of thunder rolled out of the hills, and Mr. Son Graham standing in front of the funeral home dropped a Seven-Up bottle.

The seasons drifted by. I grew six inches between the tenth and eleventh grades, and people claimed I was growing so fast I buzzed like a bee. We learned how to kiss and fondle the beautiful girls in the back seats of cars, which we parked near the cemetery or out beyond the Illinois Central tracks in the delta side of town. We stopped going to Sunday School. We drove into the hills and found

3

a secret clearing which we had almost forgotten from our child-hood and drank ice-cold beer and smoked cigarettes. The town boys had grown up together and went around in a group. Bubba Poindexter. Billy Bonner. Hershell Meade. Ed Wilburn Walters. Cotton Simmons. Kayo Fentress. "Hans" Weems. Our girls were the town girls from the best old families.

I mentioned that the town was poor. That is only partly true. We were delta people and depended on cotton, so the town was poor one year and rich the next, and everything pertained to mortgage. The planters lived in fine houses in town and rode out to their land every day in khakis like hired hands. One thunderstorm too many, or three days without rain at a critical moment, could be disastrous. That was why the talk of the weather was not a social form but an obsession, for our people were gamblers against the eternal ele-ments. The young people from the country who came to school from out of the hills were poor. The hill-country boys made good tackles and guards and centers. The town boys were backs and ends, and the town girls were majorettes and cheerleaders. I would not have used the word then, but we all had pride. It was a quirky-proud town.

One afternoon when I was fifteen I was sitting alone at the counter of the drug store after a movie—*To Have and Have Not,* with Humphrey Bogart and Lauren Bacall. It was the middle of the summer and the drug store was somnolent as the town. All of a sudden two cars parked in front. One was a new Buick sedan, the other a new Oldsmobile convertible. I noticed the big decals on both cars etched in black and gold, which said: "Jackson Central High." Four couples of high school age came inside. The boys lorded it all over the country girl who worked at the soda fountain. They were expensively-dressed in the casual Southern way. The girls wore shiny shorts and tight blouses and flitted around the jukebox, pouring in a mountain of nickles.

"Play some Tony Bennett!" one of the boys shouted from the counter.

"Hell no, play some Nat King Cole!" another demanded. I rec-ognized him. I had seen his picture several times in the sports sec-tion of the Jackson *Daily News.* He was a tailback.

From the mirror I saw them sit down at a table, where they drank their cherry cokes and whispered fun of the people who drifted in and out of the drug store. Then they ordered milkshakes, and hot dogs, and onion rings, and kept putting nickles in the jukebox. Eventually they got up to leave. They started to stroll down main street. I followed at a discreet distance.

"What a funny little town," one of the girls said. I hated her golden beauty, her honeyed hair.

Then they returned to their cars. I stood alone under the shade of the awning of Mr. Chewing Gum Fulgate's tire store watching them. Mr. Fulgate joined me. "Who are them kids?" he asked.

"They're from Jackson Central High, " I said.

"Damned snobs!"

One of the boys threw a balled-up chewing gum wrapper at an old colored man who was propped asleep against the side of Jitney Jungle. Then the two cars disappeared around Broadway.

I saw the same tailback again on a Friday afternoon that fall. It was one of those cool, windswept days of late October, and Billy Bonner and Bubba Poindexter and I were waiting in the service station at the top of Broadway while they repaired the water-pump on Billy's old robin's-egg blue Chevy. Three bright new buses pulled in for gas, painted in black and gold with "Central High of Jackson" on their sides.

"They're headed into the delta," Billy said. "They're playing Greenville tonight."

As the buses departed, I saw the tailback sitting on the front row of one of them. He and his friends looked down at us. They grinned and gave us the finger.

Our senior year arrived soon enough. I remember the news from Korea on the radio.

That year they brought in a new football coach. His name was "Blackie" Piersall, a big chunky young man who had played with Charlie Conerly, Barney Poole, and Farley Salmon at Ole Miss. The first thing he did was install the split-T formation.

In my junior year I had made the travelling squad under Coach

"Aussie" Austin, who wore glasses and had three fingers on his left hand, but I failed to earn a letter. I was the third-team wingback in the single-wing offense and only got in on seven plays all season. We finished with two wins and eight losses, including a 50-7 debacle at the hands of Belzoni, and they got rid of "Aussie" Austin, whose reputation in his three years was for cursing at his players with florid, unheard-of four letter words and for paying too much attention to the girls in his forestry class. He had also broken out a window of our dressing room with a football shoe after our 20-0 loss to Indianola.

Despite the fact that he sang bass in the Episcopal choir, Coach Blackie Piersall was a rigid taskmaster. During our torrid two-a-day practices late that summer at Poindexter Field, as we suffocated in the 100-degree heat and ran our interminable wind-sprints, he told us this would be "The Year of the Choctaws." I would go home at sunset and sit for a long time in a hot bath, nursing my bruises and drinking gallons of water.

"Did you drink a lot of water when you got home yesterday?" he once asked me.

"No sir," I lied.

"Well, don't do it. Water's no good for you in this weather."

"You fellows are used to the single-wing," he lectured us right at the start. "The split-T's a whole new ball game. It's revolutionized a slow old sport. It's designed for a small, quick, run-oriented offense. It don't give you much time. You gotta be quick, quick! Don't tarry. Move around at all times." And with that he would send us off on ten more windsprints in the broiling dust.

Even before school opened, Central High of Jackson loomed before us, a monstrous negation of our hopes. It would be our ninth game, the next-to-last one. As the season began, we read every Saturday in the supercilious Jackson papers of the exploits of the Central Tigers. By the time of our first game, against Indianola at home, I was the second-team right halfback behind Billy Bonner. We lost to Indianola, 21-14, under the pale lights of our field before two thousand spectators and three million delta bugs who were drawn in out of the bottoms by the illumination, while Jackson Central was destroying Natchez, 48-0. "A big cat playing around with a little mouse," the Jackson papers said of Jackson Central High and Natchez, not only ignoring the fact that Natchez had humiliated Belzoni 60-12 in the same year Belzoni beat us 50-7, but ignoring too the noble and patrician history of that city by the River, which I had read about in a book loaned to me by Mrs. Idella King and called *The Old Natchez Lineage* by Priscilla Jumper Tankersly.

I did not even play in that first game. I was skinny, six feet and one hundred and fifty pounds, and people made fun of my legs. I was the third fastest member of the squad, behind Billy Bonner and Bubba Poindexter, but I could not knock down a toothpick. Yet it was not merely the thing to do to be on that team, even though I was not especially good at it. More than ritual was at stake. There was the matter of duty and honor, although I did not perceive it that way in those days, of course.

Oh, but I remember that golden Indian summer, and the delicious, bittersweet throbs of love—Katie Culpepper, a long-legged majorette, sweet and cheery and lush, a fount of loyalty and fun. I had just won the high school spelling bee, a marathon that lasted six straight weekly assemblies, culminating in a lengthy *mano a mano* with Marion Whittington which put everyone to sleep until, after two hours and twenty minutes, as we lobbed words back and forth between us as lazily as tennis balls on a summer's day, a subtle electricity seized the atmosphere of the auditorium and all the bored boys and girls in the flush of creamy Mississippi adolescence suddenly opened their eyes and stirred to life when Mrs. Idella King pronounced the word *sacrilegious*. Divine irony intervened when I snared Marion Whittington, son of a pastor, on just such a word. I believe even Coach Blackie Piersall was impressed.

And so was Katie Culpepper, who hugged me right in the hallway outside the auditorium and whispered: "My darling boy." Katie, who would go anywhere and do anything—sit with me on her front porch and watch the cars go by, or play me her records, or drive the backroads on smoky afternoons, or dance close to the words of Jo Stafford with her fingers casually on the lobe of my ear, or ask if I was happy and what could she do to make me happier, or explain to me why she was a connoisseur of Dr. Peppers and strawberry milkshakes, or study her books with me on school evenings and ask for help. . . .Katie, my straight-C scholar of deep embraces and warm moist kisses, a childlike face and woman's hips and full ripe breasts that became mine long before that long-ago night against Central High of Jackson.

Leaves of a dozen colors drifted down out of the trees in those sad and wistful days, those sad, horny delta days. We remember what we wish to remember; it is all there to be summoned, but we pick and choose—since we are what we are—as we must and will. Katie and I are standing in the side lawn of her house, under an ancient water chestnut. She has been showing me her baton-twirling tricks, picked up at the Ole Miss Baton-Twirling Clinic. She is still tanned from the summer sun, her long blond hair is bobbed at the back, and her green eyes twinkle in mirth. I lean across and kiss her gently on the lips, and she kisses me in return. We stand in a light, amiable embrace; her cheek brushes mine. Oh, sweet agony of the loins! Bubba and Billy suddenly speed by in Billy's Chevy, Debbie and Laura Jane in tow, and shout greetings at us, and the leaves arc aimlessly from the trees, and there is a hazy crispness in the air. I gaze down from the summit of a quarter of a century, living in the Kingdom of the Yankee, all the accumulated losses and guilts and shames and rages, the loves come and gone, and *death*, ravenous death, and I summon now that instant standing in the shade of the chestnut with Katie Culpepper, herself long dead, buried under a mimosa on the hill in our cemetery far away, and I am caught ever so briefly in a frieze of old time, skinny and tall and seventeen, and the senior year stretching before me as a Lewis Carroll dream, beckoning: "Come, lad."

Artifice, all of it. They were burying the Korean dead. And Jackson Central two months away.

The next week, again at home, we edged Leland, 14-13, to the margin of Hershell Meade's extra points, as I acquired splinters on the bench and Bubba Poindexter ran eighty-two yards for one touchdown and thirty-six for another with college scouts in the grandstand. However, the grizzly and prematurely aging country boys in our line would not block, and the band played off key. We got our senior rings that day, and at the dance after the game I gave mine to Katie, who put adhesive tape on the inside and wore it on her index finger.

That next Friday we were on the road against Belzoni, a tough cotton hamlet forty miles into the delta, a cotton-gin and honky-tonk town nestled on the same murky river as ours. I should describe this road trip in some detail, not only because it was a small presage of things to come, but because I learned something from it, one of those life's lessons a young man is supposed to get from football, as Coach Blackie Piersall and everyone else said.

We had a rickety old bus, painted in our colors, red and black, with "The Choctaw" on both sides. That Friday afternoon we boarded "The Choctaw" in front of the school building. The students came out to send us off. The band played the fight song, and the cheerleaders and majorettes pirouetted under the somber skies. They would all follow us into the flat land later in the day. I waved goodby to Katie, and with a rattle of gears we were off to the Tenderloin Grill at the top of the hill for a pre-game meal of roast beef and mashed potatoes.

No sooner had we gotten on "The Choctaw" again than it began to rain, a hard relentless Mississippi rain that would not stop for a long time.

It certainly had not stopped well into the third quarter against the rugged, sinister Belzoni boys before twelve or fourteen hundred drenched spectators on the field behind their school. I sat on the edge of the bench under an umbrella Katie had brought me from the bleachers, sharing it with Gene Autry Simms, our second-team guard. Although the Belzonians had already lost their first two games, they were unyielding against us as always, and they weighed two hundred pounds from tackle to tackle. I was ashamed of my clean uniform. The Belzoni fans shouted curses at my comrades toiling in the precarious mud of that field, ignoring Gene Autry and me.

A succession of disasters struck in that quarter. Billy Bonner fractured his little finger, but Blackie Piersall kept him in. Cotton Simmons, the right end, took an underhanded blow to the lip and was led off with a mouth the size of a grapefruit. He was treated by Dr. Tommy Gilruth, who came and sat next to him on the bench and asked him what day it was. Cotton later told us he did not know what *state* we were in, so much for the day. Ed Wilburn Walters sprained his ankle on a pass pattern in the flat. "Hans" Weems, substituting for Ed Wilburn, was cleated in the neck. Kayo Fentress was knocked unconscious by a gang tackle and did not wake up until the fourth quarter. Big Ruby Mitchell broke his nose and was replaced at fullback by Juice Coody. Leroy Hipps, our biggest man at tackle (later second-team all-Southeastern Conference at Mississippi State) broke two fingers on two different plays. Everyone else on that filthy, moiling turf sustained bad bruises in that quarter, and there was blood mixed in with the delta ooze. On the bench I smeared some of the mud on my jersey. At that moment the loudspeaker gave some outside scores. Jackson Central 53, Biloxi 12.

And it was close. With three minutes remaining in the game Belzoni was ahead 19-14, but we had the ball at midfield. A Belzoni partisan threw a bottle toward our huddle and was led away by two state troopers. Our band broke into the fight song.

Suddenly Billy Bonner staggered to our bench with a gash on his elbow. Blackie Piersall motioned to me. I threw down my umbrella as he yanked me by the arm. "Tell Hershell Tear-Left." There was a strange glint in his eye.

I raced onto the field, almost slipping in the mud, and gave the play to Hershell Meade. "Tear Left" was a quick pitch to Bubba Poindexter at left halfback, with the left tackle, Leroy Hipps, leading interference around left end and the right halfback—myself— feinting into the line. Our flanker, "Hans" Weems, went in motion to the right and the fullback, Juice Coody, filled the hole where Leroy pulled. If "Hans" did a good job hookblocking the defensive end, we had a chance for long yardage. As I hit a tangle of Belzoni linemen, I heard a roar from our side of the field. Bubba picked up his blockers and gained eighteen yards to the Belzoni 32-yard line. In the huddle Hershell called the same play. This time Bubba went to the 24. Second and two, two minutes ten seconds to play.

Billy Bonner appeared from nowhere in the huddle and pulled at my jersey. Dr. Gilruth had poured iodine on his cut, and so much for me. I ran off the field and got my umbrella back from Gene Autry Simms. I felt a drop of blood on my cheek. I allowed it to stay there.

Billy Bonner straight ahead for seven. First and ten on the Belzoni 17. Juice Coody up the middle for three. Second and seven on the 14. One minute, twenty-seven seconds. Bubba Poindexter on the pitchout option for six. Third and one on the 8. Bubba on the quick-opener for three. First and goal on the 5.

Through the mist and rain the bedraggled scoreboard showed forty-seven seconds to play. Billy Bonner for one on the right side. Bubba Poindexter for one on the quick-opener. Third and goal from the three. Fourteen seconds to play.

Hershell Meade called time out. Blackie Piersall shouted for Gene Autry Simms. We all crowded around in the rain to listen. "56-B, end zone buttonhook, got it Gene Autry? *Got it, Gene Autry?*" Coach Piersall sometimes complained that Gene Autry forgot the plays between the bench and the huddle. Gene Autry, who stuttered, nodded his big head and entered the battle.

Our cheerleaders were soggy silhouettes as they gazed out onto the field. Mr. "Chewing Gum" Fulgate, sitting in the middle of a group of merchants, seemed in an attitude of prayer. The high school principal, Mr. Terry Buffaloe, had both arms raised with his fists clenched, and Mrs. Buffaloe was hiding her eyes with her hands.

We broke from the huddle, Hershell Meade barking the signals. Hershell faded back with the snap. There, as sweet and effortless as a Mozart minuet, all alone a few yards deep into the end zone on the buttonhook, was Billy Bonner. An easy lob by Hershell, and Billy had it. Four seconds to play, 20-19. Hershell booted the conversion, Belzoni went nowhere on the final kickoff, and that was it.

I have failed to explain that Coach Blackie Piersall was gentler than he seemed. In fact, as the season progressed, perhaps out of our mutual adversity, he actually grew more kind-hearted, and even more intelligent. Normally he would have let our girls, the majorettes and cheerleaders, ride back home with us on "The Choctaw." But everyone was too hurt for that. After we had dressed in near stony silence in the dreary visitors' locker-room populated by roaches, we limped onto the bus. I rolled down my window and took Katie's hand. The other girls flocked around the faithful "Choctaw," cooing to the wounded: "Good game, Billy. . .Good game Hershell. . .Good game, Ed Wilburn." "Good game," Katie said, and blew me a fine kiss.

As Blackie Piersall started the motor and Dr. Tommy Gilruth handed out aspirin, I noticed Billy Bonner reaching outside his window for a sizeable object. Billy's daddy was handing him up a case of beer.

Blackie Piersall also saw this, but said nothing, as Billy distributed the sweet nectar of Jax to his teammates. The bus rattled through the desolate streets of Belzoni and onto the flat, straight highway home. Except for a few moans and short, clipped curses, no one said much of anything. Cotton Simmons' mouth, though the swelling had subsided, looked ghastly. Kayo Fentress appeared dizzy. Big Ruby Mitchell gingerly touched his nose. Leroy Hipps looked down at his fingers. The rain had stopped now, and a ghostly mist rose from the black land all around us. The stalks of dead cotton stretched interminably away, and the delta bugs began to splatter against the windshield.

The second beer was even better than the first, sending mellow waves all through me. I leaned back in my seat and gazed out at the great sweep of the land in the darkness.

At that moment, with no warning, Billy Bonner stood up from the back seat of "The Choctaw," breaking the long silence.

"Well, boys," he shouted, flourishing his bottle of Jax with his undamaged hand, and everyone turned to look at the valiant little figure standing there. *"Boys, we won!. . .We won, by God.We won away from home in the last minute!"*

I suppose we knew, Billy and Bubba and Hershell and all of us, that Belzoni would be among our finest hours.

That Saturday night, for the midnight show at the Rebel it was

A Place in the Sun with Liz Taylor and Montgomery Clift. Katie and I chose not to double-date with Billy Bonner and Debbie. When a couple, new to one another, was getting "serious," they would go it alone. We parked on Cemetery Hill. Do you remember, Katie? It *was* starting to get serious, wasn't it?

As for the Choctaws, we had our vicissitudes leading to the November 22 mismatch with Jackson Central. We lost to Drew the next week, 20-14, then tied Batesville 14-14 and beat West Tallahatchie 20-12. Then on consecutive Fridays at home we were trounced by Kosciusko 32-14 and Cleveland 27-7. Coach Blackie Piersall sent me into all of these games, but never for more than three or four routine plays. I carried the ball six times for a net gain of twelve yards. Billy Bonner was firmly entrenched at right halfback, Hershell Meade was the best punter in the D.V.C., and at left half, despite our ignominious record, Bubba Poindexter—six feet, 195, and 10-flat in the hundred—was being touted for All-State.

The Saturday morning after the Cleveland debacle, several of us were lounging in the sunshine in the park. We had the Jackson paper. The banner headline in the sports section read:

Jackson Central Outclasses Greenville 48-0

And the smaller headline underneath:

Throwaway Game Friday
Before Vicksburg Showdown

"Throwaway game!" Billy Bonner said in disgust. He snatched the paper from Hershell Meade and perused the article. Then he read the Jackson record out loud to us. I still have that clipping. It is here before me now as I write these words, all shrivelled and yellow.

Jackson Central	48	Natchez	0
Jackson Central	34	Meridian	7
Jackson Central	53	Biloxi	12
Jackson Central	41	Tupelo	7
Jackson Central	47	Memphis Central (Tenn.)	7
Jackson Central	34	Gulfport	0
Jackson Central	55	Hattiesburg	0
Jackson Central	48	Greenville	0

Katie was lying in my lap looking up at the clouds. Debbie was painting her toenails. Bubba and Laura Jane were reading the front page of the paper about the war. Hershell was flexing his fingers where he had been stepped on the night before. In a moment Hooker, a tall colored boy who went to the Number Two High School, ambled by on the sidewalk with a lawn rake over his shoulder.

"Hey, Hooker!" Billy Bonner said. "I heard you got stomped yesterday by Durant. How come you let little ol' Durant do that?"

"Yeah," Hooker said. "I heard *you* got stomped by little ol' Cleveland. Ain't you *ashamed?*"

"We'll whip you Number Two boys any time, Hooker," Billy said.

Billy's antagonist was some distance beyond us now. "Who y'all playin' next week anyhow?" he shouted. "What's the name of that town? You needs me! You needs somebody to catch a pass, not bobble it like a egg. You got guys who can't catch a *watermelon*." And he laughed crazily.

"Can *you* catch it, Hooker?"

"Oh yeah, can I catch it! Can *you* catch it?"

Billy shouted a curse, and Hooker hooted some more, then vanished around Calhoun Street.

Something was snapping in Billy Bonner, having to do with the strain of the season, perhaps, or the challenge awaiting us next Friday, or maybe a profounder concern, although I always doubted if Billy were any different on the inside from what he was on his surface.

"That one looks like God," Katie said.

"*What* looks like God?" Billy demanded.

"That big cloud up there."

"Damn you, Katie, you're dumb."

I looked up at the cloud, and sure enough it *did* look like God, if you approached it from a certain angle.

"And what's that *book* you got there?" he asked me.

"It's a library book," I said. Billy picked it up and examined it.

It was called *The Sun Also Rises* by Ernest Hemingway.

"What's it about?" he asked.

"I don't know."

"It's got to be about something besides the sun rising," he persisted.

In truth, I was having a hard time with that book. "Well," I replied, "it's about. . . .losing."

"Losing!" Billy said.

"Yeah," Hershell Meade interjected. "We're experts on that,"

Billy slammed down the book and left to go squirrel-hunting with his cousins in Panther Creek.

He had been gone no more than a few minutes when the funeral procession came by—one of the country boys several grades ahead of us, brought back now from Korea. The long obsidian hearse reflected the morning's sun as it led the cars slowly on its journey to the cemetery. We watched silently as the sad parade went by, then talked a little about the boy, who was only a wisp out of a distant past for us. When the last car turned left on Lamar, we got up to leave.

That afternoon Katie and I took her mother's car and, just to get out of town, drove down to Vicksburg. It was chilly and clear on the drive south over the last finger of the delta, and the land was flooded from the rains until we reached the hills. On the radio we had the Ole Miss-Tennessee game from Memphis, then we switched to the dance music from WWL. The haunted town on the River bluffs drowsed in the autumn sun and gave an aura of age and suffering and faint riverboat decadence. We rode up and down the steep inclines past the mansions half-hidden by towering magnolias and the courthouse which had somehow survived the shellings. Out in the battlefield, we walked through the endless rows of Union gravestones. The ground was heavy with fallen leaves, the squirrels danced about everywhere, and out in the distance was the echo of a train's whistle.

We drove by the gullies and ravines and the hilly terrain dotted with the monuments to the top of the bluffs. We got out and sat on the steps and looked toward the River at the far horizon, shimmering in the November gold. I had my arm around Katie, and suddenly some Yankee tourists appeared from beyond the rampart, saying cheery hellos and leaving us to our privacy. We sat there for a long time, watching as the River turned to deep shades of brown with the sun's descent.

"What are you thinking about?" she asked.

"A lot of things. . .How much I want the season to end, I guess."

"Will you go with me next year—to Ole Miss?"

"I'll try."

"I want you with me."

"I know that."

"And. . ." She looked at me with her impish green eyes. "I'm ready now for. . .you know."

"Oh. You are?"

"Yes."

"Hey!"

"Will you find us a place? Vicksburg's a big old town."

A curious thing happened that next week, not unfamiliar perhaps to the human species. Even in the certainty of defeat, the town became obsessed with the Friday night game, as if pride itself, indulged before the fact, would dampen the ashes of sorrow. It was said that about half the white population would travel the sixty miles in private cars and several chartered Southern Trailways buses. The director of the band had ordered new saddle-oxfords for all the musicians, assessing them five dollars apiece for this acquisition. The cheerleaders had been preparing a special set of acts for several days, to culminate in a dissolving pyramid of flesh, girls somersaulting to the ground at perfect three-second intervals. Huge hand-lettered, red-and-black signs appeared overnight all over town, sponsored by the Kiwanis Club and Fulgate's Tire Store, saying: "Go Get 'Em, Choctaws!" There was an unexpected demand for red and black crepe paper in Woolworth's and Kuhn's. Our Jewish mayor, Mr. Fred O. Fink, issued a proclamation urging support of the team "against an unnamed metropolis sixteen times larger than ours." In response to an article by the sports editor of the Jackson *Clarion-Ledger* suggesting that the scheduling of the game was a travesty and asking the cadre of Jackson Central coaches to give their regulars the night off, Billy Bonner's father wrote a personal letter telling the editor precisely where to place his column, and at what angle. On Sunday, by prearrangement, the pastors of the Baptist, Methodist, and Presbyterian churches offered prayers involving the traditions of the town and the school and the gallant and unblemished Christian allegiances of both. The Episcopalians, it was rumored, would have joined this display of strength but felt it out of character with *their* traditions, so they would charter a bus for their parishioners instead. The Boy Scout and Cub Scout troops were going en masse in their uniforms. "The Choctaw" got its first washing and greasing of the season, and the local weekly, *The Sentinel,* ran a front-page headline accompanying the team picture: "Brave Little Choctaws Face Big City Boys."

If the truth be known, Katie and I met three times that week at the noontime break, skipping cafeteria, in a secret place behind the Brickyard Grove. She went out the back door of the school and walked up Filmore and Calhoun the quarter of a mile to the bayou. I left through the front door and went up Davis, taking a shortcut through several backyards to the grove. Our rendezvous was the cool secret glade of cedars by the creek, a bosky glade of my childhood.

Later, sitting on her front porch after football practice that Monday, I could have cared less about a game, even this one. I only wanted to be with Katie. She took my hand and told me the majorettes were putting small battery flashlights on each end of their batons for the game. "Isn't it exciting?" she asked. "Aren't you excited?"

"No," I said.

I felt guilty about discouraging her enthusiasm, for I would have done anything for Katie that day. But that afternoon Coach Blackie Piersall had given us an expert's description of the Jackson Central squad, which averaged two hundred and twenty pounds from end-to-end. They had held their opponents, the aristocrats of the Mississippi gridiron, to sixteen first downs all season! They

17

worked from a single-wing offense and were three-deep in all positions. Their entire starting team, he said, would play in college.

Coach Piersall had led us to a fetid, isolated spot under the grandstand, having chased away the three or four dozen spectators who had come out of curiosity, or masochism, to observe our preparations. "We're just coming out full-throttle," he said. "A lot of passes and pitch-outs, and leave the big line alone if possible." He went on to explain that he was installing three or four unusual new plays that he had not taught us before now because he did not think we could handle them, but that we had nothing to lose anyway. Johnny Vaught at Ole Miss had used these plays only in the direst emergency, he said. One, for instance, was a double reverse with the right halfback eventually passing all the way across the field to the left end. Another was called "Sprint Left," which was a pass play where the key man was the fullback, Big Ruby Mitchell. He brush-blocked the defensive end and slipped downfield as a receiver. The quarterback, Hershell Meade, had the option of running or throwing, depending on what the end did. If the end dropped back to cover Big Ruby, Hershell ran. If he committed to containment, Hershell threw long to Big Ruby. "This is a dandy play," Blackie Piersall said. "But I ain't sure you're up to it. What the hell? We'll try it. Anyhow, you can't use it but once."

"Above all," he shouted under the grandstand that day, "hold your heads high! And remember Belzoni! And don't read the damned Jackson papers!"

There was, in fact, a wonderfully infectious spirit to the practices later that week—not unlike, I imagined, the Japanese Kamikazi pilots I had read about from World War II, and the ceremonies they had before they took off in their Zeroes.

On Thursday, Principal Buffaloe came on the loudspeaker. "Because we want you to get to Jackson for the game early tomorrow evening," he said, "and not have to rush too much and get all reckless, school will be dismissed at noon." The rest of his remarks, which invoked the Lord, went unheeded before the cheers and claps and whistles which reverberated through the old building from every classroom, a wild and reckless incantation that could have been heard in the fishing boats on the river.

Friday came, and it was cold. A frigid wind had sprung up from the delta. The sky was a hard, brittle blue.

We went through the motions of morning classes. Mrs. Idella King read to us from Tennyson:

"Tho' much is taken, much abides;
One equal temper of heroic hearts,
Made weak by time and fate, but
strong in will
To strive, to seek, to find, and not
to yield.

I was following the words from the textbook, and I noticed she left out the following lines after "abides:"

And tho'
We are not that strength which
in old days
Moved earth and heaven, that
which we are, we are—

Moments after the noon bell, the school was strangely deserted, except for the band, which tarried to practice Sousa marches from its quarters in a reconverted quonset hut behind the school, and the majorettes, who were rehearsing their routines outdoors to the tune of the marches. Blackie Piersall had gotten the managers to lay out pallets on the basketball court so we could rest in the early afternoon. Many of the team dozed there in their sock feet, and Big Ruby Mitchell snored horrendously through his broken nose from the Belzoni game. Others stretched out and talked in nervous whispers. Coach Piersall, who had been helping the managers load the uniforms, came into the gymnasium and everyone was quiet again. Then he went back outside.

Ed Wilburn Walters, on the next pallet, nudged Billy Bonner and me and pointed to the large set of windows at the far end of the court. There was Debbie, who had climbed onto something to reach the high window outside and was waving in to Billy, and Billy waved back. Momentarily Laura Jane appeared there and waved at Bubba Poindexter. When she vanished, my heart skipped a throb, for my heart was telling me who would be there next, and there she was, Katie, so pert and lovely and I had to take a deep

19

breath as she smiled at me through the glass. Then she too was gone.

Blackie Piersall shouted at us to get up and put on our shoes. On a blackboard in the center of the basketball court he stressed the important Jackson Central offensive plays again. Next, for the twentieth time, he diagrammed the new plays he had installed for us.

Then we were off in "The Choctaw," stopping at the Tenderloin Grill again for the roast beef and mashed potatoes, and heading now up and down the hills covered with seared kudzu, through the sleepy impoverished little Mississippi hamlets in the chilled sunshine toward toward our appointment. Cars with red-and-black streamers sped past, blowing their horns, and the passengers waved enthusiastically. The chartered bus filled with the Boy Scouts roared by, and they let down their windows and cheered, their driver sounding the bus horn to the exact beat of the fight song. Soon the bus carrying the band slipped in behind us and blew *its* horn, and it stayed right there all they way, as a cruiser might escort a stricken destroyer to port. I knew Katie was back there somewhere.

The shadows of late autumn fell on the forlorn hills, and the trees and even the telephone poles covered with the creeping kudzu were tossed in grotesque silhouettes. In the outlaying town of Pocahontas the street lights were already on. Then we rounded a bend and were at the outskirts of the immense city which Sherman had burned years and years ago, and which had risen up again long before we were born and was waiting for us now.

Far in the distance the State Capitol loomed before us, illuminated with flood lights, like a picture-postcard against the darkening sky.

There are some things which come back in memory as in a dream. Psychiatry reminds us that dreams tell us who we are. I myself have learned that many of the ineffable moments of life— moments of grief or ecstacy or suffering, of love or triumph or sorrow—are dream-like in their unfolding, at once softer and more stark than reality itself.

So it was for me that night in the big stadium off State Street. What was it but a dream?

I remember the deafening noise from the crowd as we lined up at the entranceway under the stadium. We wore black jerseys with white numerals, and black-and-red pants and helmets. The half-backs and ends wore low-quarter shoes, the linemen full-quarter ones, and our cleats rattled on the concrete as we waited there, jumping up and down to keep warm. I looked down at my jersey, Number 22, and across at Bubba Poindexter's, Number 24, and for no reason at all I recalled my first memory of Bubba. We were four years old and I was killing ants with a hammer on the sidewalk in front of my house, and Bubba said: "The Lord ain't goin' to like that." Now, wordlessly, Bubba and I bumped our shoulder-pads together to get them straight.

Then, on Blackie Piersall's signal, we rushed through the entranceway onto the lush green field. The cheers from our towns-people seemed pathetic in the vast structure, so horrifically outnumbered by the thousands of Jackson Central partisans, and our band was as reedy and offkey as it had always been. An eerie autumnal half-moon had ascended out beyond the field lights, and when the Jackson Central squad appeared from the opposite end of the stadium, big and swift and menacing in their flashy black-and-gold, the roar from the stands and the brassy beat of the prodigious band and the yells of three or four dozen cheerleaders who led them out and the explosion of a small cannon in their end-zone made one's very footfalls on the grass of the turf inaudible. There truly were about seventy-five of them, and under the giddy beams of light with the stands rising high into the night they seemed of sufficient numbers to have overrun McClellan at Sharpsburg.

Soon Bubba Poindexter and Hershell Meade were at midfield shaking hands with the Jackson captains—one of them a lineman of at least six and a half feet—and Bubba and Hershell ran back to the rest of us waiting in a semi-circle in front of our bench. We

21

had won the toss of the coin and would receive from the north goal. We gathered around Blackie Piersall and recited *The Lord's Prayer,* and then stood at attention for *The Star-Spangled Banner.* When that was over our band began the fight song, but no sooner had they played three or four bars than the Jackson band drowned them out with theirs.

In the course of human events, as all mystics comprehend, there can be a magic, defying all logic, which will seize a moment, something absurd and indeed existential, undergirded by old unfathomable mysteries—the eternal enigmas of the Old Testament, for instance—and this, of course, is the material of poets. On that faraway night, in the instant the Jackson kicker let fly his long end-over-end kick, there had to be a poet's soul in Bubba Poindexter as he stood waiting on our five-yard-line.

Bubba took the ball in his chest and moved swiftly to the left side, then slowed ever so briefly to watch the lay of the blocking. Of this there was practically none. The Jackson defense was speeding down in his direction like behemoths, knocking over the entire left flank of our kickoff phalanx, and in one startling moment Bubba turned at a complete angle on the 15-yard-line and reversed his field, making a rounded arc in the wrong direction as he did so. One Jackson player hit him on the ankle on the 25 and he stumbled before regaining his balance, but miraculously the whole right side of the field opened up with the exception of a mammoth end who was rushing in to cut Bubba off near the sidelines. From nowhere came Leroy Hipps, who chopped the end to earth with a jarring block.

That was all there was to it. Bubba sped by me only a yard or two away on the bench—I could have reached out and touched his jersey—staying just inside the boundary, the entire gridiron empty before him. When he reached the opposite end zone, there was not a Jackson player within twenty-five yards. A few seconds after that, Hershell Meade split the uprights for the extra-point.

The human animal needs time to digest experience. It had all happened too fast, consuming about as many seconds as it may have taken the reader to read the previous two paragraphs. Even our own players did not respond unduly to Bubba's 95-yard touchdown. Two or three of them may have slapped him on the back as they returned to the huddle for Hershell Meade's extra point, but there were no shouts or wild embracings. In fact, when Bubba crossed their goal, the Jackson thousands seemed still to be cheering from the adrenalin of the opening kickoff, and our outnumbered loyalists desperately needed a moment or two to absorb that to which they had just been witness. By the time of Hershell's conversation, however, a silence impenetrable as death had settled upon the Jacksonians while our students and townspeople, so indiscriminately crowded in the lower seats behind our bench, sent forth a terrific roar that would have frightened hearty attack dogs away, and began hugging one another as if their lives depended on it.

Jackson Central made two quick first downs after the ensuing kickoff, and then ground to a halt. Something enigmatic was transpiring in the interior line. Unbelievable as it may seem, our linemen were fighting them down, clawing them down like beasts fighting for survival. Outweighed twenty pounds to the man, Leroy Hipps and Big Boy Hendrix and the others were not merely standing their ground, they were penetrating that awesome singlewing blocking, bleeding and cursing and gang-tackling, and opening tiny crevices on offense for Bubba Poindexter and Billy Bonner and Big Ruby Mitchell to squirm through. On a third and twenty Bubba gained twenty-eight yards on one of Blackie Piersall's new secret plays. Big Ruby got fourteen on another new play. But these were the only substantial gains for either side, and at the end of the first quarter, the score stood 7-0.

Time passed swiftly in the second period. Neither team could move the ball consistently, and that strange game settled down into exchanges of fourth-down punts. I had known Hershell Meade since he first started kicking footballs in the second grade, and he had never kicked better. The vicious, crushing action largely was taking place between the two 30-yard-lines.

A mounting tension suffused the atmosphere, not orgiasmic now, but a subtle deepening of emotion. We were holding them! Billy Bonner even intercepted one of their passes on our 40-yard-line in that quarter, and Cotton Simmons burst through later and threw the Jackson tailback, fading for a pass, for an eighteen-yard loss. Unaccustomed to such rude treatment, the Jackson players resorted to venomous curses and taunts. Two fist-fights erupted, and "Hans" Weems was penalized fifteen yards for hitting his opposite number with clenched fists after his adversary had elbowed him in the groin, the original transgression having been missed by the referees. Our foe was also having difficulties with penalties, on one late hit and three clips. Given the ferocity of play at the line, it was surprising there were no serious injuries. Big Ruby Mitchell lost a tooth to go with his broken nose, Kayo Fentress sustained a gash on his forearm, Cotton Simmons had an index finger dislocated, and Hershell Meade had to come out for two plays feeling giddy, but when he realized he was on the sidelines, he ran back into the fray without so much as conferring with Blackie Piersall.

Plainly it was the element of surprise which was making the Jackson Central team so sluggish. Had they played the role of Mississippi bully for too many seasons? Near the end of the first half, when their tailback was crushed out of bounds on their 28-yard-line by Leroy Hipps and "Hans" Weems for a six-yard loss and three or four of their players came to help him to his feet, from my spot on the bench I saw the expression of astonishment in their eyes. Not hurt, only incredulity, the way General Hooker must have looked at Chancellorsville when he gazed to his rear and sighted Stonewall's emaciated, barefoot infantrymen coming up fast. I knew enough football, too, to perceive that Blackie Piersall was relying now on his innate conservatism. With notable exceptions, little of the histrionic action he had said we would need had been summoned. The second quarter, as with most of the first, was a matter of pitiless bone-crushing.

A funny emotion had seized certain sections of the big stadium. With two minutes remaining in the half, I looked around and noticed that more and more people here and there were cheering our team. At first I was baffled by this phenomenon, but then I perceived what it was. The hundreds of small-town people who had come to observe the unchallengeable Jacksonians were reverting to their origins. They sensed a historic vengeance. They were with us.

I heard a yell from the back of the bench. The band was coming down for its half-time performance. There was Katie, shivering in her tight majorette's uniform, the flashlights twinkling on each end of her baton. "Isn't it wonderful?" she shouted; then she vanished in the throng.

Soon the gun sounded for the first half, with us in possession on our own 31-yard line. The score was 7-0.

Blackie Piersall was unexpectedly subdued in the locker room at half time, in fact almost a benign presence, going over some of the enemy's favorite offensive plays and defensive alignments on the blackboard, and the team was as quiet as he, resting for the mighty drama ahead. Coach Piersall's only concession to the accumulating tension came when we got up to leave. "Just remember," he said. "You can tell your grandchildren about this!"

The third quarter began as the second had ended, unspectacular exchanges between the thirty-yard-lines, small gains, and fourth-down punts. As the minutes ticked by, however, I saw that our opponents' coaches were beginning to dispatch more and more substitutes from their untapped reservoir of manpower. I overheard Blackie Piersall whispering to Dr. Tommy Gilruth: "They're gonna try to wear us down."

There were two minutes, 47 seconds left in the third quarter and we had a first and ten from our own 29 when it finally happened. Billy Bonner took a pitch-out from Hershell Meade and was skirting left-end when two Jackson linemen upended him with an agonizing tackle which could he heard all the way across the field.

Billy did not get up.

Blackie Piersall and Dr. Tommy Gilruth rushed out and bent over Billy Bonner. They stayed there a long time. Bubba Poindexter and Big Ruby Mitchell helped him off the field. Already his ankle was swollen to twice its size. "For Christ's sakes, don't touch the damned thing," Billy cried as they laid him out behind the bench.

The moment had come, as I knew it might, as if my entire seventeen years had been building toward it. Blackie Piersall called my

25

name. I went over to him as I strapped on my helmet, walking as calmly as I could to disguise the dreadful turmoil inside.

"Just take it easy," he said. "Tell Hershell 68-B left. We'll start you right off."

Sixty-eight-B left was the right halfback's call.

Need it be said that what one sees on the field is a world apart from the bench? The hatred in the eyes of the enemy linemen, the whispered threats, the falsetto squeals of pain, the fatigue etched deeply in the faces of one's teammates were larger than mere life. The dream had taken over again.

Sixty-eight-B was a quarterback pitchout with the right halfback sweeping wide to the left. Before I knew it, Hershell Meade had faked to Big Red Ruby at fullback and then the pitch was coming out to me. I took it at a canter and followed two blockers. Suddenly the broad swathe of daylight which had appeared in the left-flat closed. Three huge Jackson defenders attacked from all sides. I fell with a crash to the soft earth. When I got up I felt numb, yet all the nervousness had dissolved. I had gained seven yards!

Gene Autry Simms ran in from the sidelines to the huddle. "S-s-same play!" he ordered. "S-s-same damned p-p-play!" This time I took the lateral from much farther out. Hershell's aim was not as accurate as before, but I had it at the knees. The whole left side of our line was holding off the front defenders. There was a large opening now off to the center, and beyond that, where the linebackers were being staggered by fierce blocks, another empty space flickered in the corner of my eye. I moved in that direction, picking up speed as I ran. An enemy defensive back was closing in from the left, but "Hans' Weems appeared before me to brush him aside, and I was momentarily free, moving easily and alone as in the races we once had at recess in grammar school. Out of the old inexplicable instincts of one born to run fast I cut toward the left sidelines, until another defensive back struck me from the right, and I kept going until I stumbled out of bounds. I got up again and looked around. We were on their 33-yard-line. I had gained thirty-two yards.

Blackie Piersall was sending in every play now. Bubba on the quick-opener for three. Big Ruby on a trap for one. Bubba on a pitchout for one. The third quarter ended with us on their 30-yard line, fourth down and five to go.

We went to the opposite end of the field for the huddle. Gene Autry galloped in again. "S-s-seventy-four-B extra s-s-special," he said.

"Again?" Hershell Meade asked him.

"S-s-seventy-four-B extra s-s-special."

"Are you sure?" Hershell persisted.

"F-f-fuckin'-A, I'm sure," Gene Autry said. "Y-y-you think I'd s-s-screw up now?"

Seventy-four-B extra special was one of the new plays, the double-reverse with the right halfback finally getting the ball, stopping in his tracks on the far left side and passing all the way across the field to the end deep. We had practiced it all week.

"Can you handle it?" Hershell asked me.

"I'll try," I said.

We moved from the huddle. Then the play began to unfold, Bubba Poindexter shoving the football squarely into my stomach as I dashed to the right. I stopped. Two tacklers were heading toward me. As I gazed downfield, everything seemed to move in slow, unhurried, exaggerated motions, belabored and unreal. I even remember seeing the eerie half-moon, and under it, all alone and waving frantically to me, gyrating all over like a man in the throes of a seizure was my friend from kindergarten on—Ed Wilburn Walters, the number on his jersey, 88, standing out sharp and clear. I cocked my arm and threw the ball in his direction, farther it seemed than I had ever thrown anything in my life, so that my whole right arm tingled with the effort, the way one feels when he hits his funny-bone on the edge of a hard object, and at that instant the two tacklers plummeted into me, and I crashed again to the ground. A few seconds later, one of the Jackson tacklers, who was still half-sitting on me, said: "Shit!"

By the time I was upright, Bubba Poindexter raced over and pounded me on the back. So did Hershell and Big Ruby. A fervid din rose from our spectators.

"What happened?" I asked.

"He caught it, you fool!" Bubba said. "Right on the goal-line. Only end-over-end pass I ever saw."

Hershell's kick was perfect once more, and we led 14-0 with fourteen minutes, forty-two seconds left in the game.

Blackie Piersall would not use me on defense. Instead he put "Hans" Weems in the defensive backfield where Billy Bonner had been. As I sat there again on the bench, I understood now what our coach had meant about the enemy's substitutes. There was a whole new group on almost every play. As for us, the ceaseless pounding without relief was beginning to take its toll. Our players moved slowly after every play.

This draconian fatigue showed when the enemy's second-team offense gradually moved upfield after our kickoff. Wide gaps in our defense elicited runs of twenty, fourteen, and seventeen yards, and a screen-pass went for twelve. With 10:41 to play, as if an afterthought, they scored on a post-pattern from our 11-yard-line, adding the point to make it 14-7.

In the huddle when our turn came, there were groans and pained breathing. "Them bastards are dirty as Belzoni," Leroy Hipps said. Yet we managed two first downs, the second coming on a five-yard gain by me to our own 44. On a fourth and eight from our 48, "Hans" Weems replaced me, and I watched from the bench as Hershell Meade booted a long, true spiral to the Jackson seven. One of their vast corps of halfbacks gathered in the ball and started upfield. Our bench cried in misery as he broke open on his 30. Cotton Simmons, the only man between him and the goal, succeeded in bringing him down on our 34. Seven plays later they scored on a short pass into the flat. They kicked the point.

The score was 14-14 with 5:36 left to play.

Again we could not move the ball. I was thrown for a four-yard loss on the same 68B which had succeeded earlier. Big Ruby Mitchell was stopped for no gain. Bubba Poindexter took a short pass from Hershell Meade and sprang free for seventeen yards to our 43-yard-line. But that was all. With 4:20 to go, the intrepid Hershell Meade kicked out of bounds on the enemy's 12-yard-line.

From the bench I heard now a sound unlike any I had ever heard before, a vast rhythmic roar, filling the Mississippi night under its

28

stark November half-moon. It had an unearthly resonance, cruel and smug and old as time, an unholy incantation against all of us who have ever been outnumbered, and tired, and in pain, and a long way from home. "*Go. . . Go. . . Go. . . Go. . . !*" The thousands of Jackson partisans were standing, stretching their arms and gesturing in unison, encouraged by the slow, erotic beat of their drums and cymbals, and the yells of their many women, and the echo of their momentous chant resounded off the facades of both sides of the stadium and merged on the field where we stood. "*Go. . . Go. . . Go. . . Go. . . !*"

Our foe marched from the huddle. Four up the middle. Seven on a buttonhook. Six on a power right. Nine on a power left. Five on a buttonhook. Eleven on a screen pass. The big scoreboard showed one minute, 59 seconds to play and Jackson had a first and ten on our 47-yard-line. They were moving now, and they knew it, with their fresh, undirtied recruits, bludgeoning our line, riddling our secondary with short swift passes.

The Jackson tailback faded for another pass. Far downfield, behind "Hans" Weems, one of their ends was breaking clear. The tailback poised to throw. As he did so, in the very moment of throwing long, Leroy Hipps crashed through two blockers and brushed the tailback's shoulder. The ball hovered for a moment in mid-air, just beyond the line of scrimmage, wobbling like a dying bird in flight, and as it fell earthward Ed Wilburn Walters with one prodigious effort swooped toward it, embracing it with both arms in a passionate gesture of belonging. Then he fell to the turf. At first we could not see, because his back was to us, but the referees made their motions and everyone helped Ed Wilburn to his feet.

He had intercepted the ball on our 46-yard-line. One minute, 48 seconds to play.

Everything came swifter now, in a blur of tangled bodies and brute flailings. Big Ruby for seven to the Jackson 47. Bubba Poindexter for six and the first-down on the Jackson 41. "Belzoni!" Bubba whispered in the huddle. Then, almost tenderly: "*Remember Belzoni?*"

"Sprint Left," the last new play, came in from the bench. Big Ruby Mitchell would slip deep downfield, Hershell Meade having the option of running or throwing, depending on what big Number 86, the defensive end, did. Hershell took the snap and dashed to the left, eluding a throng of tacklers, then against every dictum in the book, faded back. It was almost a failed play. He heaved. Lying prone on the ground, I peered through the night. Big Ruby Mitchell leapt higher and higher, far over the torso of a lone defender. He came down with the ball on the 7-yard-line.

One minute even remained, as we called time-out and gathered in the huddle. Everyone was gasping for air. Blood streamed out of the sleeve of my jersey. Hershell Meade had a nasty, battered eye. Leroy Hipps had a jagged cut under his nose. Bubba Poindexter stared across at me without expression. The stadium was now ghostly silent, like a sepulcher. An insane thought ran through my brain, from my readings in Mrs. Idella King's class. Someone would dig this all up someday and surmise: there seemed to have been a public meeting-place here.

Gene Autry Simms interrupted my demented reverie. "Forty-two-A." It was Bubba Poindexter's call, the standard split-T quick-opener up the middle.

In the split-T, it must be said here, which was perfected by Don Faurot at Missouri and refined by Bud Wilkinson at Oklahoma and Johnny Vaught at Ole Miss in the late 1940's (and become long-since outmoded) the fullback lined up directly behind the quarterback three yards deep. The left-and right-halfbacks were positioned on either side of the fullback, also three yards deep. On the quick-opener, at the snap of the ball from the center to the quarterback, or on the signal for the snap—*Ready* or *Set* or *One* or *Two* or *Three* or *Four*—the two halfbacks would rush straight out of their pointed stance for the line of scrimmage. In our lexicon, on "42-A" the quarterback would hand off to the left handback heading directly toward the middle of the opposing line, crashing through it behind quick, precise blocking. On "42-B" the hand-off was to the right halfback on exactly the same pattern.

Now we are in the huddle. Hershell crouches before us. *"42-A— Off on Set."* We go to the line. Hershell bends behind Big Boy Hendrix at center. Now he shouts: "Ready. . . *Set!*" The play unfolds with breathless precision. Bubba batters through the enemy line for three yards, to the four-yard-line.

Fifty seconds.

Once more we are in the huddle. Cotton Simmons comes in from the bench and is standing before us. "Forty-two-B."

"Again?" I ask.

"Forty-Two-B."

And Hershell: *"42-B... Off on One."*

We break the huddle, taking the familiar pointed stance. Is anything what it ever seems to be? There is one final, all-meaning silence as Hershell kneels behind the center. Then: "Ready... Set... *One!*"

I hurdle ahead, feeling the whack in my abdomen. For the merest instant I feel the clawing of desperate boys, the hammer of big adolescent bodies, and then as I pitch forward a terrible blow to my midriff spins me off-course, and I am plummeting downward into an abyss of flesh.

Only when I hit the earth do I sense I am no longer holding the ball. It is bouncing crazily to my right, out of the range of the manswarm which entraps me. I reach helplessly for it, reach out very far, but it is gone from me, irretrievably and forever. As it settles on the one-yard-line, just before the enemy end pounces lovingly upon it, I see the contrast between the brown of the ball and the deep green of the grass.

I awakened in my bed the next morning to the memory of it. People were not as bad as they could have been. After all, some of them volunteered, we tied Central High of Jackson.

But I saw it in their eyes. Some of my friends avoided me in the dressing room. Leroy Hipps shook his head when he saw me. Blackie Piersall patted me on the back and went on with his duties, but his eyes were unforgiving. One of the Jackson coaches, who had come over to shake hands with Blackie Piersall, bent down with a whiskey-breath and whispered, "Thanks, kid." Some of our townspeople, waiting outside as we walked to "The Choctaw," turned away as I passed.

She was waiting for me, Katie, in a little circle of shadows near "The Choctaw." I could tell she had been waiting for me there in the cold for a long time. She embraced me. "My poor sweet boy," she whispered as she held me. "Did they hurt you?"

I could sense the look. When I went to see Billy Bonner in the hospital, I could tell even he was not saying what he wanted to say. Hershell and Bubba were with me in Billy's room, and Hershell said he did not remember a thing after the blow he got on his head in the second quarter. "I didn't know nothin' until. . .you know." Then he turned to me. "Hey, I'm sorry. I shouldn't have said that." I would walk up unannounced to a group of people, and there would be awkward silences. The men in the barber shop were not themselves when I came in.

It was Katie who got me through the next few days.

One afternoon a month later, however, a still weekday afternoon with no one about, I was walking down the deserted main street on an errand from school for Mrs. Idella King. Suddenly, from far behind me, I heard the word boom out at me:

"Butterfingers!"

I whirled around. There was no one in sight

At the high school graduation that May, when Principal Buffaloe handed me my diploma and announced I had beaten Marion Whittington by two-tenths of a grade-point and was the valedictorian, he looked at the audience in the gymnasium, where we had rested on pallets that day before driving to Jackson, and added: "So you see, we forgive him his little. . .*mistake.*" Everyone laughed and applauded.

One hot day in late August I went to say goodby to Katie, who was leaving for Ole Miss. It was the last time I ever saw her.

"I'll always love you," she said. "I'll see you Christmas."

"Christmas," I repeated.

"I'll forgive you not going with me. Didn't I adore you even after the. . .?" She paused.

"Fumble!"

"But, my baby," she said, leaning into me as she always would, smiling at me with her green eyes. "It was only a game."

That's what they always say. Even Katie—God bless my precious Katie—did not believe it. Not in that place, and in that time. Up there on the gold-paved streets of heaven, with free Dr. Peppers and strawberry milkshakes running perpetually out of the very water taps, she is looking down at me. She is whispering to me. What is it, my Katie? Speak to me before you fade from me forever, speak to the long-ago boy who loved you. I strain now to hear her words. . . . "My poor sweet butterfingers."

The Phantom
of Yazoo

To Warner Alford, Dog Brewer, and Lee Hunt

LIKE MARK Twain and his comrades growing up a century before in another village on the other side of the Mississippi, my friends and I had but one sustaining ambition in the 1940s. Theirs in Hannibal was to be steamboatmen, ours in Yazoo was to be major-league baseball players. In the summers, we thought and talked of little else. We memorized batting averages, fielding averages, slugging averages, we knew the roster of the Cardinals and the Red Sox better than their own managers must have known them, and to hear the broadcasts from all the big-city ballparks with their memorable names—the Polo Grounds, Wrigley Field, Fenway Park, the Yankee Stadium—was to set our imagination churning for the glory and riches those faraway places would one day bring us. One of our friends went to St. Louis on his vacation to see the Cards, and when he returned with autographs of Stan Musial, Red Schoendienst, Country Slaughter, Marty Marion, Joe Garagiola, and a dozen others, we could hardly keep down our envy. I hated that boy for a month, and secretly wished him dead, not only because he took on new airs but because I wanted those scraps of paper with their magic characters. I wished also that my own family were wealthy enough to take me to a big-league town for two weeks, but to a bigger place even than St. Louis: Chicago, maybe, with not one but two teams, or best of all to New York, with

36

three. I had bought a baseball cap in Jackson, a real one from the Brooklyn Dodgers, and a Jackie Robinson Louisville Slugger, and one day when I could not even locate any of the others for catch or for baseball talk, I sat on a curb on Grand Avenue with the most dreadful feelings of being caught forever by time—trapped there always in my scrawny and helpless condition. *I'm ready, I'm ready,* I kept thinking to myself, but that remote future when I would wear a cap like that and be a hero for a grandstand full of people seemed so far away I knew it would never come. I must have been the most dejected looking child you ever saw, sitting hunched up on the curb and dreaming of glory in the mythical cities of the North. I felt worse when a carload of high school boys halted right in front of where I sat, and they started reciting what they always did when they saw me alone and day-dreaming: *Wee Willie Winkie walks through the town, upstairs and downstairs in his nightgown.* Then one of them said, "Winkie, you *gettin'* much?" *"You bastards!"* I shouted, and they drove off laughing like wild men.

Almost every afternoon when the heat was not unbearable my father and I would go out to the old baseball field behind the the armory to hit flies. I would stand far out in center field, and he would station himself with a fungo at home plate, hitting me one high fly, or Texas Leaguer, or line drive after another, sometimes for an hour or more without stopping. My dog Skip would get out there in the outfield with me, and retrieve the inconsequential dribblers or the ones that went too far. I was light and speedy, and could make the most fantastic catches, turning completely around and forgetting the ball sometimes to head for the spot where it would descend, or tumbling head-on for a diving catch. The smell of that new-cut grass was the finest of all smells, and I could run forever and never get tired. It was a dreamy, suspended state, those late afternoons, thinking of nothing but outfield flies as the world drifted lazily by on Jackson Avenue. I learned to judge what a ball would do by instinct, heading the way it went as if I owned it, and I knew in my heart I could make the big time. Then, after all that exertion, my father would shout, "I'm whupped!" and we would quit for the day.

When I was twelve I became a part-time sportswriter for the

Yazoo Herald, whose courtly proprietors allowed me unusual independence. I wrote up an occasional high school or Legion game in a florid prose, filled with phrases like "two-ply blow" and "circuit-ringer." My mentor was the sports editor of the *Memphis Commercial Appeal,* whose name was Walter Stewart, a man who could invest the most humdrum athletic contest with the elements of Shakespearean tragedy. I learned whole paragraphs of his by heart, and used some of his expressions for my reports on games between Yazoo and Satartia, or the other teams. That summer when I was twelve, having never seen a baseball game higher than the Jackson Senators of Class B, my father finally relented and took me to Memphis to see the Chicks, who were Double-A. It was the farthest I had ever been from home, and the largest city I had ever seen; I walked around in a state of joyousness, admiring the crowds and the big park high above the River, and best of all, the grand old lobby of the Chisca Hotel.

Staying with us at the Chisca were the Nashville Vols, who were there for a big series with the Chicks. I stayed close to the lobby to get a glimpse of them; when I discovered they spent all day, up until the very moment they left for the ballpark, playing the pinball machine, I stationed myself there too. Their names were Tookie Gilbert, Smokey Burgess, Chuck Workman, and Bobo Hollomon, the latter being the one who got as far as the St. Louis Browns, pitched a no-hitter in his first major league game, and failed to win another before being shipped down forever to obscurity. One afternoon my father and I ran into them outside the hotel on the way to the game and gave them a ride in our taxi. I could have been fit for tying, especially when Smokey Burgess tousled my hair and asked me if I batted right or left, but when I listened to them as they grumbled about having to get out to the ballpark so early, and complained about the season having two more damned months to go and about how ramshackle their team bus was, I was too disillusioned even to tell my friends when I got home.

Because back home, even among the adults, baseball was all-meaning; it was the link with the outside. A place known around town simply as The Store, down near the train depot, was the principal center of this ferment. The Store had sawdust on the floor and long shreds of flypaper hanging from the ceiling. Its most familiar staples were Rexall supplies, oysters on the half shell, legal beer, and illegal whiskey, the latter served up, Mississippi bootlegger style, by the bottle from a hidden shelf and costing not merely the price of the whiskey but the investment in gas required to go to Louisiana to fetch it. There was a long counter in the back. On one side of it, the white workingmen congregated after hours every afternoon to compare the day's scores and talk batting averages, and on the other side, also talking baseball, were the Negroes, juxtaposed in a face-to-face arrangement with the whites. The scores were chalked up on the blackboard hanging on a red and purple wall, and the conversations were carried on in fast, galloping shouts from one end of the room to the other. An intelligent white boy of twelve was even permitted, in that atmosphere of heady freedom before anyone knew the name of Justice Warren or had heard much of the United States Supreme Court, a quasi-public position favoring the Dodgers, who had Jackie Robinson, Roy Campanella, and Don Newcombe — not to mention, so it was rumored, God knows how many Chinese and mulattoes being groomed in the minor leagues. I remember my father turned to some friends at The Store one day and observed, "Well, you can say what you want to about that nigger Robinson, but he's got *guts*," and to a man the others nodded, a little reluctantly, but in agreement nonetheless. And one of them said he had read somewhere that Pee Wee Reese, a white Southern boy, was the best friend Robinson had on the team, which proved they had chosen the right one to watch after him.

There were two firehouses in town, and on hot afternoons the firemen at both establishments sat outdoors in their shirt-sleeves, with the baseball broadcast turned up as loud as it would go. On his day off work my father, who had left Cities Service and was now a bookkeeper for the wholesale grocery, usually started with Firehouse No. 1 for the first few innings and then hit Number Two before ending up at The Store for the post-game conversations.

I decided not to try out for the American Legion Junior Baseball team that summer. Legion baseball was an important thing for country boys in those parts, but I was too young and skinny. My main concern that summer lay in the more academic aspects of the game. I knew more about baseball, its technology and its ethos, than all the firemen and Store experts put together. Having read most of its literature, I could give a sizable lecture on the infield-fly rule alone, which only a thin minority of the townspeople knew existed. Gentleman Joe was held in some esteem for his strategical sense, yet he was the only man I ever knew who could call for a sacrifice bunt with two men out and not have a bad conscience about it. I remember one dismaying moment that came to me while I was watching a country semi-pro game. The home team had runners on first and third with one out, when the batter hit a ground ball to the first baseman, who stepped on first and then threw to second. The shortstop, covering second, stepped on the base but made no attempt to tag the runner. The man on third had crossed the plate, of course, but the umpire, who was not very familiar with the subtleties of the rules, signaled a double play. Sitting in the grandstand, I knew that it was not a double play at all and that the run had scored, but when I went down, out of my Christian duty, to tell the manager of the local team that he had just been done out of a run, he told me I was crazy. This was the kind of brainpower I was up against.

That summer the local radio station started a baseball quiz program. A razor blade company offered free blades and the station chipped in a dollar, all of which went to the first listener to telephone with the right answer to the day's baseball question. If there was no winner, the next day's pot would go up a dollar. At the end of the month they had to close down the program because I was winning all the money. It got so easy, in fact, that I stopped phoning in the answers some afternoons so that the pot could build up and make my winnings more spectacular. I nettled about $25 and a ten-year supply of double-edged, smooth-contact razor blades before they gave up. One day, when the jackpot was a mere two dollars, the announcer tried to confuse me. "Babe Ruth," he said, "hit sixty home runs in 1927 to set the major-league record. What man had the next-highest total?" I telephoned and said, "George

Herman Ruth. He hit fifty-nine in another season." My adversary, who had developed an acute dislike of me, said that was not the correct answer. He said it should have been *Babe* Ruth. This incident angered me, and I won for the next four days, just for the hell of it.

On Sunday afternoons we sometimes drove out of town and along hot, dusty roads to baseball fields that were little more than parched red clearings, the outfield sloping out of the woods and ending in some tortuous gully full of yellowed paper, old socks, and vintage cow shit. One of the backwoods teams had a fastball pitcher named Eckert, who didn't have any teeth, and a fifty-year-old left-handed catcher named Smith. Since there were no catcher's mitts made for left-handers, Smith had to wear a mitt on his throwing hand. In his simian posture he would catch the ball and toss it lightly into the air and then whip his mitt off and catch the ball in his bare left hand before throwing it back. It was a wonderfully lazy way to spend those Sunday afternoons—my father and my friends and I sitting in the grass behind the chicken-wire backstop with eight or ten dozen farmers, watching the wrong-handed catcher go through his contorted gyrations, and listening at the same time to our portable radio, which brought us the rising inflections of a baseball announcer called the Old Scotchman. The sounds of the two games, our own and the one being broadcast from Brooklyn or Chicago, merged and rolled across the bumpy outfield and the gully into the woods; it was a combination that seemed perfectly natural to everyone there.

I can see the town now on some hot, still weekday afternoon in mid-summer: ten thousand souls and nothing doing. Even the red water truck was a diversion, coming slowly up Grand Avenue with its sprinklers on full force, the water making sizzling steam-clouds on the pavement while half-naked Negro children followed the truck up the street and played in the torrent until they got soaking wet. Over on Broadway, where the old men sat drowsily in straw chairs on the pavement near the Bon-Ton Cafe, whittling to make the time pass, you could laze around on the sidewalks—barefoot, if your feet were tough enough to stand the scalding concrete—watching the big cars with out-of-state plates whip by, the driver hardly knowing and certainly not caring what place this was. Way up that fantastic hill, Broadway seemed to end in a seething mist—little heat mirages that shimmered off the asphalt; on the main street itself there would be only a handful of cars parked here and there, and the merchants and the lawyers sat in the shade under their broad awnings, talking slowly, aimlessly, in the cryptic summer way. The one o'clock whistle at the sawmill would send out its loud bellow, reverberating up the streets to the bend in the Yazoo River, hardly making a ripple in the heavy somnolence.

But by two o'clock almost every radio in town was tuned in to the Old Scotchman. His rhetoric dominated the place. It hovered in the branches of the trees, bounced off the hills, and came out of the darkened stores; the merchants and the old men cocked their ears to him, and even from the big cars that sped by, their tires making lapping sounds in the softened highway, you could hear his voice, being carried past you out into the delta.

The Old Scotchman's real name was Gordon McLendon, and he described the big-league games for the Liberty Broadcasting System, which had outlets mainly in the South and the Southwest. He had a deep, rich voice, and I think he was the best rhetorician, outside of Bilbo and Nye Bevan, I have ever heard. Under his handling a baseball game took on a life of its own. As in the prose of the *Commercial Appeal's* Walter Stewart, his games were rare and remarkable entities; casual pop flies had the flow of history behind them, double plays resembled the stark clashes of old armies, and home runs deserved acknowledgment on earthen urns. Later, when I came across Thomas Wolfe, I felt I had heard him before, from Shibe Park, Crosley Field, or the Yankee Stadium.

One afternoon I was sitting around my house listening to the Old Scotchman, admiring the vivacity of a man who said he was a contemporary of Connie Mack. (I learned later that he was twenty-nine.) That day he was doing the Dodgers and the Giants from the Polo Grounds. The game, as I recall, was in the fourth inning, and the Giants were ahead by about 4 to 1. It was a boring game, however, and I began experimenting with my father's short-wave radio, an impressive mechanism a couple of feet wide, which had an aerial that almost touched the ceiling and the name of every major city in the world on its dial. It was by far the best radio I had ever seen; there was not another one like it in town. I switched the dial to short-wave and began picking up African drum music, French jazz, Australian weather reports, and a lecture from the British Broadcasting Company on the people who wrote poems for Queen Elizabeth. Then a curious thing happened. I came across a baseball game—the Giants and the Dodgers, from the Polo Grounds. After a couple of minutes I discovered that the game was in the eighth inning. I turned back to the local station, but here the Giants and Dodgers were still in the fourth. I turned again to the short-wave broadcast and listened to the last inning, a humdrum affair that ended with Carl Furillo popping out to shortstop, Gil Hodges grounding out second to first, and Roy Campanella lining out to center. Then I went back to the Old Scotchman and listened to the rest of the game. In the top of the ninth, an hour or so later, a ghostly thing occured; to my astonishment and titillation, the game ended with Furillo popping out to short, Hodges grounding out second to first, and Campanella lining out to center.

I kept this unusual discovery to myself, and the next day, an hour before the Old Scotchman began his play-by-play of the second game of the series, I dialed the short-wave frequency, and, sure enough, they were doing the Giants and the Dodgers again. I learned that I was listening to the Armed Forces Radio Service, which broadcast games played in New York. As the game progressed I began jotting down notes on the action. When the first four innings were over I turned to the local station just in time to get the Old Scotchman for the first batter. The Old Scotchman's account of the game matched the shortwave's almost perfectly. The Scotchman's, in fact, struck me as being considerably more poetic than the one I had heard first. But I did not doubt him, since I could hear the roar of the crowd, the crack of the bat, and the Scotchman's precise description of foul balls that fell into the crowd, the gestures of the base coaches, and the expression on the face of a small boy who was eating a lemon popsicle in a box seat behind first base. I decided that the broadcast was being delayed somewhere along the line, maybe because we were so far from New York.

That was my first thought, but after a close comparison of the two broadcasts for the rest of the game, I sensed that something more sinister was taking place. For one thing, the Old Scotchman's description of the count on a batter, though it jibed 90 percent of the time, did not always match. For another, the Scotchman's crowd, compared with the other, kept up an ungodly noise. When Robinson stole second on shortwave, he did it without drawing a throw and without sliding, while for Mississippians the feat was performed in a cloud of angry, petulant dust. A foul ball that went over the grandstand and out of the park for short-wave listeners in Alaska, France, and the Argentine produced for the firemen, bootleggers, farmers, and myself a primitive scramble that ended with a feeble old lady catching the ball on the first bounce to a mighty roar. But the most revealing development came after the Scotchman's game was over. After the usual summaries, he mention that the game had been "recreated." I had never taken notice of that particular word before, because I lost interest once a game was over. I went to the dictionary, and under "recreate" I found, "To invest with fresh vigor and strength; to refresh, invigorate (nature, strength, a person or thing)." The Old Scotchman most assuredly invested a game with fresh vigor and strength, but this told me nothing. My deepest suspicions were confirmed, however, when I found the second definition of the word—"To create anew."

So there it was. I was happy to have fathomed the mystery, as perhaps no one else in the whole town had done. The Old Scotchman, for all his wondrous expressions, was not only several innings behind every game he described but was no doubt sitting in some air-conditioned studio in the hinterland, where he got the happenings of the game by news ticker; sound effects accounted for the crack of the bat and the crowd noises. Instead of being disappointed in the Scotchman, I was all the more pleased by his genius, for he made pristine facts more actual than actuality, a valuable lesson when the day finally came that I started reading literature. I must add, however, that this appreciation did not obscure the realization that I had at my disposal a weapon of unimaginable dimensions.

Next day I was at the short-wave again, but I learned with much disappointment that the game being broadcast on shortwave was not the one the Scotchman had chosen to describe. I tried every afternoon after that and discovered that I would have to wait until the Old Scotchman decided to do a game out of New York before I could match his game with the one described live on short wave. Sometimes, I learned later, these coincidences did not occur for days; during an important Dodger or Yankee series, however, his game and that of the Armed Forces Radio Service often coincided for two or three days running. I was happy, therefore, to find, on an afternoon a few days later, that both the short-wave and the Scotchman were carrying the Yankees and the Indians.

I settled myself at the short-wave with notebook and pencil and took down every pitch. This I did for four full innings, and then I turned back to the town station, where the Old Scotchman was just beginning the first inning. I checked the first batter to made sure the accounts jibed. Then, armed with my notebook, I ran down the street to the corner grocery, a minor outpost of baseball intellection, presided over by my young Negro friend Bozo, a knowledgeable student of the game, the same one who kept my dog in bologna. I found Bozo behind the meat counter, with the Scotchman's account going full blast. I arrived at the interim between the top and bottom of the first inning.

"Who's pitchin' for the Yankees, Bozo?" I asked

"They're pitchin' Allie Reynolds," Bozo said. "Old Scotchman says Reynolds really got the stuff today. He just set 'em down one, two, three."

The Scotchman, meanwhile, was describing the way the pennants were flapping in the breeze. Phil Rizzuto, he reported, was stepping to the plate.

"Bo," I said, trying to sound cut-and-dried, "you know what I think? I think Rizzuto's gonna take a couple of fast called strikes, then foul one down the left-field line, and then line out straight to Boudreau at short."

"Yeah?" Bozo said. He scratched his head and leaned lazily across the counter.

I went up front to buy something and then came back. The

45

count worked to nothing and two on Rizzuto—a couple of fast called strikes and a foul down the left side. "This one," I said to Bozo, "he lines straight to Boudreau at short."

The Old Scotchman, pausing dramatically between words as was his custom, said, "Here's the windup on nothing and two. Here's the pitch on its way—There's a hard line drive! But Lou Boudreau's there at shortstop and he's got it. Phil hit that one on the nose, but Boudreau was right there."

Bozo looked over at me, his eyes bigger than they were. "How'd you know that?" he asked.

Ignoring this query, I made my second prediction. "Bozo," I said, "Tommy Henrich's gonna hit the first pitch up against the right-field wall and slide in with a double."

"How come you think so?"

"Because I can predict anything that's gonna happen in baseball in the next ten years," I said. "I can tell you anything."

The Old Scotchman was describing Henrich at the plate. "Here comes the first pitch. Henrich swings, there's a hard smash into right field! . . . This one may be out of here! It's going, going— *No!* It's off the wall in right center. Henrich's rounding first, on his way to second. Here's the relay from Doby . . . Henrich slides in safely with a double!" The Yankee crowd sent up an awesome roar in the background.

"Say, how'd you know that?" Bozo asked. "How'd you know he was gonna wind up at second?"

"I just can tell. I got extra-vision," I said. On the radio, far in the background, the public-address system announced Yogi Berra. "Like Berra right now. You know what? He's gonna hit a one-one pitch down the right-field line—"

"How come you know?" Bozo said. He was getting mad.

"Just a second," I said. "I'm gettin' static." I stood dead still, put my hands up against my temples and opened my eyes wide. "Now it's comin' through clear. Yeah, Yogi's gonna hit a one-one pitch down the right-field line, and it's gonna be fair by about three or four feet — I can't say exactly — and Henrich's gonna score from second, but the throw is gonna get Yogi at second by a mile."

This time Bozo was silent, listening to the Scotchman, who described the ball and the strike, then said: "Henrich takes the lead off second. Benton looks over, stretches, delivers. Yogi swings." (There was the bat crack.) "There's a line drive down the right side! It's barely inside the foul line. It may go for extra bases! Henrich's rounding third and coming in with a run. Berra's moving toward second. Here comes the throw! . . . And they *get* him! They get Yogi on the slide at second!"

Before Bozo could say anything else, I reached in my pocket for my notes. "I've just written down here what I think's gonna happen in the first four innings," I said. "Like DiMag. See, he's gonna pop up to Mickey Vernon at first on a one-nothing pitch in just a minute. But don't you worry. He's gonna hit a 380-foot homer in the fourth with nobody on base on a full count. You just follow these notes and you'll see I can predict anything that's gonna happen in the next ten years." I handed him the paper, turned around, and left the store just as DiMaggio, on a one-nothing pitch, popped up to Vernon at first.

Then I went back home and took more notes from the shortwave. The Yanks clobbered the Indians in the late innings and won easily. On the local station, however, the Old Scotchman was in the top of the fifth inning. At this juncture I went to the telephone and called Firehouse No. 1.

"Hello," a voice answered. It was the fire chief.

"Hello, Chief, can you tell me the score?" I said. Calling the firehouse for baseball information was a common practice.

"The Yanks are ahead, 5-2."

"This is the Phantom you're talkin' with," I said.

"Who?"

"The Phantom. Listen carefully, Chief. Reynolds is gonna open this next inning with a popup to Doby. Then Rizutto will single to left on a one-one count. Henrich's gonna force him at second on a two-and-one pitch but make it to first. Berra's gonna double to right on a nothing-and-one pitch, and Henrich's goin' to third. DiMaggio's gonna foul a couple off and then double down the left-field line, and both Henrich and Yogi are gonna score. Brown's gonna pop out to third to end the inning."

"Aw, go to hell," the chief said, and hung up.

This was precisely what happened, of course. I phoned No. 1 again after the inning.

"Hello."

"Hi. This is the Phantom again."

"Say, how'd you know that?"

"Stick with me," I said ominously, "and I'll feed you predictions. I can predict anything that's gonna happen anywhere in the next ten years." After a pause I added, "Beware of fire real soon," for good measure, and hung up.

I left my house and hurried back to the corner grocery. When I got there, the entire meat counter was surrounded by friends of Bozo's, about a dozen of them. They were gathered around my notes, talking passionately and shouting. Bozo saw me standing near the bread counter. "There he is! That's the one!" he declared. His colleagues turned and stared at me in undisguised awe. They parted respectfully as I strolled over to the meat counter and ordered a dime's worth of bologna for my dog.

A couple of questions were directed at me from the group, but I replied, "I'm sorry for what happened in the fourth. I predicted DiMag was gonna hit a full-count pitch for that homer. It came out he hit it on two-and-two. There was too much static in the air between here and New York."

"Too much *static?*" one of them asked.

"Yeah. Sometimes the static confuses my extra-vision. But I'll be back tomorrow if everything's okay, and I'll try not to make any more big mistakes."

"Big mistakes!" one of them shouted, and the crowd laughed admiringly, parting once more as I turned and left the store. I wouldn't have been at all surprised if they had tried to touch the hem of my shirt.

That day was only the beginning of my brief season of triumph. A schoolmate of mine offered me five dollars, for instance, to tell him how I had known that Johnny Mize was going to hit a two-run homer to break up one particularly close game for the Giants. One afternoon, on the basis of a lopsided first four innings, I had an older friend sneak into The Store and place a bet, which netted me $14.50. I felt so bad about it I tithed $1.45 in church the following Sunday. At Bozo's grocery store I was a full-scale oracle. To the firemen I remained the Phantom, and firefighting reached a peak of efficiency that month, simply because the firemen knew what was going to happen in the late innings and did not need to tarry when an alarm came.

One afternoon my father was at home listening to the Old Scotchman with a couple of out-of-town salesmen from Greenwood. They were sitting in the front room, and I had already managed to get the first three or four innings of the Cardinals and the Giants on paper before they arrived. The Old Scotchman was in the top of the first when I walked in and said hello. The men were talking business and listening to the game at the same time.

"I'm gonna make a prediction," I said. They stopped talking and looked at me. "I predict Musial's gonna take a ball and a strike and then hit a double to right field, scoring Schoendienst from second, but Marty Marion's gonna get tagged out at the plate."

"You're mighty smart," one of the men said. He suddenly sat up straight when the Old Scotchman reported, "Here's the windup and the pitch coming. . . . Musial *swings!*" (Bat crack, crowd roar.) "He drives one into right field! This one's going up against the boards!. . . .Schoendienst rounds third. He's coming on in to score! Marion dashes around third, legs churning. His cap falls off, but here he *comes!* Here's the toss to the plate. He's nabbed at home. He is *out* at the plate! Musial holds at second with a run-producing double."

Before I could parry the inevitable questions, my father caught me by the elbow and hustled me into a back room. "How'd you know that?" he asked.

"I was just guessin'," I said. "It was nothin' but luck"

He stopped for a moment, and then a new expression showed on his face. "Have *you* been callin' the firehouse?" he asked.

"Yeah, I guess a few times."

"Now, you tell me how you found out about all that. I mean it."

When I told him about the short-wave, I was afraid he might be mad, but on the contrary he laughed uproariously. "Do you remember these next few innings?" he asked.

"I got it all written down," I said, and reached in my pocket for the notes. He took the notes and told me to go away. From the yard, a few minutes later, I heard him predicting the next inning to the salesmen.

A couple of days later, I phoned No. 1 again. "This is the Phantom," I said. "With two out, Branca's gonna hit Stinky Stanky with a fast ball, and then Alvin Dark's gonna send him home with a triple."

"Yeah, we know it," the fireman said in a bored voice. "We're listenin' to a short-wave too. You think you're somethin', don't you? You're Ray Morris' boy."

I knew everything was up. The next day, as a sort of final gesture, I took some more notes to the corner grocery in the third or fourth inning. Some of the old crowd was there, but the atmosphere was grim. They looked at me coldly. "Oh, man," Bozo said, "*we* know the Old Scotchman ain't at that game. He's four or five innings behind. He's makin' all that stuff up." The others grumbled and turned away. I slipped quietly out the door.

My period as a seer was over, but I went on listening to the short-wave broadcasts out of New York a few days more. Then, a little to my surprise, I went back to the Old Scotchman, and in time I found that the firemen, the bootleggers, and the few dirt farmers who had short-wave sets all did the same. From then on, accurate, up-to-the-minute baseball news was in disrepute there. I believe we all went back to the Scotchman not merely out of loyalty but because, in our great isolation, he touched our need for a great and unmitigated eloquence.

Always
Stand In
Against
the Curve

To Jaybird at Sixteen

THE WAR in Korea had just started, and the radio spoke of Yaks and Stormoviks and T-34s, and Trygve Lie and Warren Austin and Sigmond Rhee. I was 17 the year we won the state championship. American Legion Junior Baseball was flourishing in the South in those days, and our team in Yazoo was an all-star club-from the whole county, an amalgam of town and country boys who played against each other during the high school season in the spring—bitter adversaries in April, reluctant allies in July. These country boys threw at your head in the springtime and came into second with their spikes high, and would not shake hands after the game. They were hard-nosed sons of the earth. Only baseball joined us, and then uneasily, and they viewed our town girls with lust and apprehension.

It was a good county for baseball, perhaps the finest in Mississippi. The Ole Miss baseball coach, one of the best in Dixie, was a Yazooan. One forlorn hamlet out in the hills would produce two pitchers for the Pittsburgh Pirates. The country boys from Satartia, Benton, Fugates, and Bentonia were tough, wily, and suspicious of the big city, Yazoo having almost nine thousand people. They read comic books, and they came to practice in the back of pick-up trucks, having worked on the farms since sun-up. They did not drink as much water as us city boys, and they were more durable in the heat. They did not like their Yazoo City teammates, thinking us soft and corrupted. They would have been in the ranks with Earl Van Dorn or N. B. Forrest in north Mississippi, or with Pemberton at Vicksburg, lean, barefoot, and hungry. They did not talk much. One of their number was a taciturn right-hander from Eden with mean eyes and the best fastball in the area. He later made Triple-A. The catcher from town would go on to star at Ole Miss, the short-stop at Mississippi State. The first-baseman's brother had just signed with the Yankees and was playing that summer with the Yankees' Class C team in Joplin, Missouri, with a fledgling short-stop he wrote his brother a postcard about which we all read, named Mantle.

Our coach was a country farmer who often complained that he was neglecting his crops. At first I thought him frivolous, with his pale eyes and his belligerent homilies, yet later I knew we would not have won without him. He quoted the Scriptures from the little concrete-block churches with impoverished graveyards far back in the woods. He had us running through the streets of Yazoo before each practice. At our field with its unpainted grandstand and pre-carious bleachers surrounded by row after row of young cotton, we lay down on our backs while he walked on our stomachs. Coca-Colas were infractions of the training rules. I can close my eyes now and smell the sharp, clean odor of the cotton poison deposited all around us by the cotton-duster mono-planes as I ran windsprints in the broiling sun.

The American Legionnaires who sponsored our team were mostly town people and had fought in World War I. They came to our practices and drove us to our out-of-town games. They were proud baseball men. One of them was my father, who had played semi-pro in western Tennessee and was nicknamed "Hooks" for the way he could hook-slide. He was thin and gaunt and was the bookkeeper for the wholesale grocery there in Yazoo City; he un-derstood as much baseball as any man I ever knew. Another was Sammy Moses, who owned the tobacco and confectionery store and whose son Gerry, our batboy, would someday spend seven years in the major leagues as a catcher with the Red Sox, Angels, Indians, and Yankees. There was Joe Bush, who ran the laundry, and Jack Barrack, a farmer, and Red Hester, who sold insurance, and Herman Nolte, who owned a service station on Broadway. As World War I men they were a dwindling cadre, for the V.F.W. was more formidable with its numerous veterans of World War II: they lived, it seemed, for baseball. They are gone now from the earth, all of them.

It was a wickedly hot summer of 1950, and the swirling dust often got in my eyes from my post in centerfield and I had to carry a wet handkerchief in my pocket. We wore white uniforms with red lettering: "Roy Lammons Post 7, Yazoo City, Miss.", and the uniforms were cheap, heavy wool, which scratched and prickled the skin until the wool became soaked in sweat.

The teams we played were Rolling Fork, Greenville, Canton, Clarksdale, Belzoni, Vicksburg, Mendenhall, and Jackson. Once we journeyed to Neshoba County to play Philadelphia; I had no inkling then of the days and weeks I would someday spend there following Marcus Dupree. We always played in the afternoons, since our field and all the others were without lights. We would be a caravan of cars making our indolent odysseys out into the delta, listening to the ominous reports from Korea or to the Old Scotchman, Gordan McLendon, doing the major league games on the Liberty Broadcasting System. At one rural field, as Sammy Moses fungoed us flies before the game, I allowed a line drive to get past me. I went to retrieve the ball in deep centerfield, a formidable terrain with mounds of junk overgrown with Johnson grass. I sighted the ball near a pile of empty bottles. As I reached down to get it, two rattlesnakes—possibly man and wife—slithered toward me. I left the ball where it was.

On another day we were driving to a game in Greenville. The American Legionnaires had provided us with a most curious vehicle—an old Pontiac sedan welded to the backside of a station wagon, so that we had a makeshift omnibus with seven rows of seats. The welding on the outside resembled nothing if not scartissue, but this conveyance actually had a motor which worked, and was big enough to accommodate the entire team and our equipment. Our country pitcher, between his perusal of a Wonder Woman comic book, jibed me for ruining his no-hitter in a game that spring with an insipid, broken-bat single into shallow right field. Far up into the delta, our coach asked me to drive. I was negotiating the flat, straight highway at fifty miles an hour when I heard the sound of cracking metal. When I pulled over to the side of the road we discovered that our omnibus had broken in two at the point of the welding, so that the middle was hopelessly collapsed, while each end pointed upward at a slant. As our coach hitchhiked to a telephone, the team assembled in a nearby cow pasture and took batting practice. After a time the coach returned with a Negro farmer in a flatbed truck. We climbed in the back and headed for Greenville. Halfway to our destination, a delta thunderstorm descended, and by the time we reached the field the whole team was drenched, our uniforms as heavy as croker-sacks. Forgiveably, perhaps, we lost that game 8-0, one of our few losses of the summer.

We drew substantial crowds to our home games. The pretty girls with double-names came to watch, sitting cool and talcumed in the shade of the grandstand, sipping the forbidden Coca-Colas. They would sit apart from the country girls unless one of the latter's fathers owned a delta plantation. Town and country people also sat in the grandstand discussing the dubious cotton crop of that season. My father and the other Legionnaires chose the bleachers behind our bench, where they conferred on strategy and advised us in whispers between innings.

By the time of the regional playoffs, our record stood at seventeen and three, two of the losses being to Jackson. The regional finals were held in Newton, Mississippi. Two of the three other teams in the tournament were exceptionally strong. Newton, the home team, had a pitcher-shortstop named Pepper Thomas, the finest athlete in the state in that day, a white Marcus Dupree, who later would reach Triple-A with the Braves. There was the omniscient Jackson, a collection of metropolitan players accustomed to winning in every sport. The fourth team, Pelahatchie, was a feeble also-ran; we had beaten them 25-0 in an exhibition game earlier in June. We were half asleep in our dormitory the night before the first day's doubleheader when our coach entered, shouting: "We drew Pelahatchie!" In the first game, we eliminated the hapless

Pelahatchians, 18-1, then got dressed in a barn that served as the fieldhouse and settled in to watch Newton and Jackson. Before the hundreds of home town followers, Jackson registered its usual victory.

Again that night, the coach came into our quarters, followed by the American Legionnaires. "You just got a telegram," Sammy Moses said. "I'm gonna read this thing to you very slow." The telegram said: "We plan to whip you country hicks so bad tomorrow you won't ever play ball again. (signed) Jackson Legion Team." Sammy Moses read the telegram once more. "Now how does *that* make you feel?" he shouted. The country boys rowsed out of their beds, revenge in their eyes. Half-naked, they ran amuck. One of them kicked over a chair. Another threw his baseball glove against the wall. "We gonna *whup* their tails!" one of them yelled, but in the ensuing pandemonium, I alone noticed the Legionnaires exchanging sly winks.

The next afternoon there must have been two thousand Newtonians at the parched little field to cheer on their small-town compatriots. The whole Newton team sat behind our bench to support us in our quest. The ersatz telegram worked. In a burst of strength, we overwhelmed our opponents, 10-4, thus winning a place in the state finals the following week.

After that, the state finals seemed anti-climactic. On a warm and luminous Saturday afternoon, before an overflow crowd, we edged Greenwood, 4-3, for the championship of all of Mississippi. My father and the other Legionnaires hastened down from the stands, awash in joy, to shake hands all around, then joined us as we posed for the team photograph at home plate.

Our next stop would be the Southern finals, to be played at the LSU field in Baton Rouge, against the championship teams from Louisiana, Texas, and Arkansas. The winner would advance to the Atlantic Seaboard tournament, and the victor there to the Little World Series, and these possibilities were exhilarating. We were good, and anything could happen. There was a two-week respite before we went to Baton Rouge. The townspeople honored us with barbequed chicken suppers, where many speeches, some solicited, were made in our honor.

Yet as in most effervescent moments, there was a vexing problem, almost Biblical in nature. The games in Louisiana would be played at night. We had never played at night before. Would this make any difference? My father and Sammy Moses said it would indeed; the ball looked different under the lights, they warned. The closest lighted field was in Silver City, out in Humphreys County in the delta. This was a most distinctive ball park, where I had gone to see many semi-pro games as a boy. It had been built right on the plantation of the Reed Brothers, "Soup" and Jack; the latter of the two would later make it to the New York Yankees. The Reeds offered to let us practice on their field. We drove there late one afternoon. The stadium was enclosed on all sides by cotton. The lights were pale on this August night amidst the smells of growing things and the sonorous delta sounds. It was difficult to tell the balls from the bugs. I dropped three or four routine flies during the practice, and everyone else did too. The coach gathered us about him during a break and advised us to forget about the lights. He led us in prayer.

A crowd was there to see us off at Mr. Herman Nolte's service station. Our coach had a new suit and new shoes. Amid little clusters of barefoot children, white and black, and the pretty girls, Mayor Harry Applebaum delivered a final soliloquy about victory and adversity.

Most of us had never been out of Mississippi before, and the arcane culture of Louisiana—they even had liquor billboards along the highways—enhanced the adventure. The grand LSU campus was like a metropolis for me. We must have made an unlikely sight in those explorations around the campus, small-town and boondocks boys and wizened American Legionnaires and the coach in his squeaky new shoes, everyone a long way from home. The empty Tiger Stadium at twilight, scene of the mighty Ole Miss-LSU games we had heard on the radio, was a fulfillment of dreams, and the baseball field set next to it made my heart beat faster for the next night's drama.

That game is etched in my memory, as indelible as first love.

We had drawn the Louisiana champions, Shreveport, in the opening round. Waxahatchie, Texas, was playing Little Rock, Arkansas, in the first match of the twi-night doubleheader, and we waited the long moments in our dormitory before donning our abrasive wool uniforms and driving across the campus to Box Field. The stadium was packed with Louisiana partisans, several thousand, who cheered the Shreveport players in their trim and fancy uniforms. Shagging flies with the others in the outfield, I again had trouble tracking the ball, which approached one not like a daytime baseball, but as a half-orb.

Later, in the dugout, I gazed across the diamond where the Louisiana pitcher was warming up. He was a little southpaw, and I was absorbed by his easy, fluid motions. He had fine speed, but it was his curveball that drew my attention. Even from that distance I could tell it was fearsome. At that age a superlative curve is an entity of its own, for one does not see very many then, and confronting a great curve at sixteen is one of life's memorable junctures, almost sexual in its intensity, and there is no full expectation of it, and no one can prepare you for it, not even yourself.

"What's his name?" I asked Mr. Herman Nolte.

"Seth Morehead," he replied.

I peered across at him again. "They told me today he's the best your age in the South," he added. "But don't let that bother you. You can hit him. Always stand in against the curve."

I hoped that was to be. But when we came to the plate in the top of the first inning and our lead-off batter, Clarkie Martin, who had never once struck out in a game of baseball, went down on three pitches, I had a premonition of what we faced. Clarkie returned to the dug-out with woebegone features. "I couldn't even *see* it," he said.

This game exists for me now in a curious blur, every movement attenuated. Our all-state shortstop dropped two pop flies. Our left-fielder mishandled a casual line drive. Our catcher, the finest in Mississippi, allowed an easy pop foul behind homeplate to elude him under the unfamiliar lights. Louisiana took a swift 2-0 lead. In the second inning with no one on base, a towering fly came out in my direction. For one terrifying moment I lost it in the lights, then caught it with a desperate hand-over-heels lunge.

I batted eighth in the order and came to the plate in the third

58

inning, carrying the Jackie Robinson Louisville Slugger my father had bought me in Jackson; it had accompanied me though the long season. I stood there in the box looking out at Seth Morehead as he gazed down at me, silent and poised. His first pitch was a slicing curve of a kind I had never seen before, so swift and deadly I could barely believe what I had just observed. "Good boy, Seth!," the big catcher shouted. "This guy's a joker." The second pitch was a hard fastball on the inside. I swung and tapped a harmless foul into the dirt. The third offering was another sharp curve which broke outside; perhaps it would be called a slider today. Whatever the name, I observed it in trepidation as the umpire called me out.

As the game progressed, we made more errors on routine plays, while out Louisianan contemporaries, who had played most of their games at night, were flawless in the field. Clarkie Martin struck out again. So did I. Yet somehow we held our own. Our heaviest country hitters, oblivious to the lights and to the drama, finally began to hit the dexterous little lefthander in the waning innings. Clarkie Martin and I both struck out a third time. Yet we trailed by only one run, 4-3, when I came up again in the top of the ninth, a runner on first and one out. This time I looked out fiercely at Seth Morehead, praying silently to the Mississippi Methodist Lord. "Please, God," I mumbled to myself, "let me hit this nighttime curve." But the first pitch was a fast ball which went by me for a strike. The second was also a fastball, low and inside, kicking the dust. I dug in with determination. Seth Morehead looked down for the signal, stretched, then threw. I caught the twist of the curve several feet out, swinging mightily, hitting a sharp line drive that winged toward left field—foul by three or four feet. I had hit him! Momentarily, my adversary, unperturbed and assured as ever, was throwing again. The blistering curve came in. I swung, missing the breaker by more than a foot. "Go home and practice," the catcher snarled. Our last batter, the country pitcher, also went down ignominiously swinging. We had lost to Louisiana. The partisan crowd roared in support.

I do not know what made me do it—certainly not "sportsman-ship," for I was much too crestfallen for that. Perhaps it was something deeper in the blood. But as the Louisiana players surrounded their victorious pitcher, and soon began to disperse, I found myself walking in their direction.

"Hey—Number Twelve—Seth. . . .Seth Morehead!" I shouted.

He looked up casually as he was putting on his jacket. "Yeah?"

"Well. . . ." I stumbled for the words. "You're great! You're a great pitcher."

"Hey!" he said. "Thanks. I appreciate it."

I noticed to my surprise that my teammate Clarkie Martin was right behind me. "Hey, Morehead!" he shouted. "Number Twelve! Why don't you come live in Yazoo next summer? I don't want to hit against *you* no more."

He grinned up at us, his victims, then extended his hand to us both. "I might do that. Hey, I appreciate it. Say, good luck tomorrow."

Playing erratically again under the lights, anything but the team that had undergone the splendid Mississippi summer, we lost the next night to Waxahatchie, Texas, as if the effort against Morehead's curveball had desecrated forever our deepest aspirations. We were eliminated. In the dormitory the American Legionnaires were bleak and dejected. The coach led us again in prayer. We drove all the way home in the somber night, several sixteen-year-olds who had learned a little about loss.

Yet as the days drifted toward the autumn, it did not seem all that bad—not truly. What if we had faced that curve ball in broad daylight in the Sovereign State of Mississippi? The merchants of town took up a collection and sent us to St. Louis for three days to see the Cardinals play the Phillies, when the catcher and I would be interviewed by Harry Carey himself on the Griesedick Brothers Beer Network. Not long after that, we got our shiny blue jackets with "Miss. State Champs, 1950," emblazoned on the back. Football arrived, and basketball, and time came and went. The town boys and the country boys pitted inexorably against each other in the next high school baseball spring did not snarl as before. It was as if we were an elite comaraderie, and when our mean-eyed pitcher from the summer induced me into a tame pop fly with the bases loaded and two out in the ninth and Yazoo a run behind on their treacherous little field, he bounded off the mound and shook my hand, saying: "I'm sorry I had to do that." That August those of us still eligible were eliminated by the same Jackson team we had beaten the summer before.

I went away to college in Texas, still playing baseball in the summers on a semi-pro squad, until the day came when I was twenty-one and played my last game. I got a scholarship to England, married an American girl, and had a son there who cost 82 cents. I lost touch with the boys of our championship year, who scattered throughout the burgeoning cities of the New South. One by one the American Legionnaires died, including my father. Baseball was far away in Oxford, England. Yet even there, in that medieval town on the Thames, a grown-man and a father, too, I had a recurring dream of my grotesque adolescent efforts to hit a curve under the lights in Baton Rouge, Louisiana.

My wife and new son and I returned to our native land in the summer of 1960, on the *Isle de France* to New York. Then we drove southward, for I had a newspaper job in Texas. We stopped briefly in Mississippi, where I made a solitary nostalgic visit to our old baseball field.

One summer Saturday afternoon, only two weeks returned to America, I was lounging on the floor in my father-in-law's house in Houston, lazily watching the Major League Game of the Day on national television; Dizzy Dean and Pee Wee Reese were calling the action. Only my six-month-old son was in the room with me, crawling about on the floor, knocking objects off tables, nibbling the cover of a *Life Magazine.* For a while I watched the game, which was between the Chicago Cubs and the Milwaukee Braves, absorbing again the satisfying old nuances of the sport I had forgotten all those years. Then I fell into a half-sleep, a mid-summer's reverie of displacement and homecoming. The words of Pee Wee Reese—something he was trying to tell me—suddenly stirred me from my lethargy.

"Now pitching for the Chicago Cubs, coming in from the bullpen. . . .the fine little southpaw Seth Morehead."

I was fully awake, sitting on my haunches. There on the screen was the imperturbable figure from that long-ago night, tossing down his fast-breaking warmup curves, while Hank Aaron watched his moves from the on-deck circle.

I looked about the room for someone to talk to. The boy was crawling around the coffee table. "Hey!" I shouted at him, so emphatically that he paused for an instant. "See that lefthander? He once struck out Clarkie Martin and me four times under the lights in Baton Rouge, Louisiana!" The infant son pondered me as if I had uttered something momentous, or taken all leave of my wits. Then he resumed his peregrinations, just as Hank Aaron took a brisk curve on the inside corner for a strike.

Bevo Goes to Notre Dame

*To Billy Ross Brown,
David Sansing, and Will Norton*

BACK IN 1954, when I was at the University of Texas, I had a friend named Dean Smith, an imperturbable Texas ranch boy who ambled along at an exceedingly slow pace and talked even slower. Dean, however, had once come close to being the fastest man in the world. In the 1952 Olympics he had placed fourth in the 100 meters. "I thought I'd won the thing," he would drawl, "but then they brought out them *pictures.*"

It seems poetic, in retrospect, that this wisp of the cinder track was also the caretaker of the official Texas mascot, a 1,500-pound longhorn steer by the name of Bevo V. This was by no means a sinecure. Dean had fallen into it not only because he had a vast and arcane expertise on cows and steers but because he was the only person on campus who could handle Bevo V.

Bevo was one mean creature. He was the fifth in the succession of heralded longhorns who reigned in Austin, making his ceremonial appearance at all the games, and it is no happenstance that he had to be replaced shortly after the episode I shall recount. O. Henry called Austin "the city of the violet crown" because of the lovely muted blue hills that touch upon it, and Bevo was quartered on a ranch out in that terrain, beyond the Balcones Fault. Lesser men than Dean Smith would drive to the ranch to see how Bevo was doing, only to return to the campus with ripped and bloodied clothes, cuts and bruises. Once, it was told, he kicked down half the side of a barn. On another occasion he got loose at a football game and terrorized the Baylor University marching band.

In the fall of '54, Texas had an important football engagement in South Bend. Early that week I ran into Dean Smith on the campus, sitting in the shade of a tree, chewing on a straw of hay and watching the coeds drift by. "Say, you want to go to South Bend with ol' Bevo and me?" he asked. "I can't get nobody to go. Nobody seems to like Bevo too much." I was an ambitious young reporter on *The Daily Texan* and could see a good story or two in the trip, so I immediately said yes. "You got to help me with ol' Bevo, though," my friend warned.

I went to a second-hand store near the capitol building and outfitted myself in a 10-gallon hat and boots. Being a Deep Southerner, I felt strangely ersatz in this apparel, and even more so when I met Dean that Wednesday. He stifled a laugh and we proceeded with the business at hand.

When we arrived at the ranch, Dean brought Bevo outside. "Now," he said, "I'll teach you how to put a rope around his neck. The most important thing is self-confidence. If he thinks you're scared, you're in big trouble. Take the rope and very slowly walk up to him, right between his horns, and look him straight in the eye. Don't fidget and don't let him stare you down. Don't pay any attention to the horns. Look him *straight in the eye.* Then, very gently, put the rope around his neck."

He demonstrated his technique three or four times, then handed me the rope. I took a deep breath, remembering my intrepid Confederate forebears, and walked up to that fine-looking behemoth. Against my better instincts I followed Dean's advice, gazing squarely into Bevo's huge liquid eyes, and slowly put the rope around his neck. "You did it!" Dean shouted. "Now he knows who you are. He may even like you. But one other thing, and don't forget it. Never make any sudden movements around him. And never, no matter what, approach him from the rear."

We put Bevo in a trailer laden with hay and equipped with an immense water bucket. With that, in a soft Texas twilight, we were off. We had decorated the trailer in orange-and-white streamers to go with the sign "BEVO V OF THE UNIVERSITY OF TEXAS." An occasional car would pass us, and the occupants, loyal Texas fans, would blow their horn and roll down their windows to give the "Hook 'em Horns" sign.

Through the night, Dean and I took turns driving. This was before interstates came to Oklahoma and the roads left much to be desired. The going was slow. Furthermore, Bevo was so big that every time he chose to shift his weight, our station wagon would move with him.

We kept on across the dry and lonesome Oklahoma plains, the bugs splattering on our windshield, our radio tuned in to WWL in New Orleans or to the gospel music from Piedras Negras, stopping now and again to let Bevo out to stretch and to allow me to file a couple of reports to my paper from the Western Unions: "With Bevo V in the Midwest."

As we approached St. Louis, the trip had begun to wear on us and we made for a motel on the outskirts of town. We tied Bevo to a tree, then marched into the office. A woman was working behind the counter.

Despite his ranch hand habitudes, Dean had unexpected moments of rhetoric and a keen feel for the histrionic. Sometimes this is in the chemistry of sprinters, a breed of individualists, as if they must repay in kind for their God-given wings. "Madame," Dean said, "this ol' boy and I are from Texas, and we're on our way to South Bend, Indiana, for the Texas-Notre Dame football game on Saturday afternoon."

The woman looked up with a bored glance. "Yes?" she asked.

"We been drivin' all last night and all today and we're awfully tired. We need a room to rest in."

"We've got plenty of vacancies," she replied.

"We'll take one," Dean went on. "The only problem is, we got a 1,500-pound longhorn steer out there tied to one of your trees."

"I'm sorry," she said, "but we don't allow pets."

We drove on, crossing into southern Illinois, fortified by enormous quantities of black coffee. Three other motels along the way refused to let us leave Bevo outside in his trailer.

"These Yankees don't appreciate top class," Dean said. Darkness had descended again, followed by a windswept rain. Dean began talking about Bevo, about how he considered him a real friend. "You see, they got him too old down at the university. He was already set in his ways. He's proud, and he don't trust too many people. And people make fun of him. That's why he got after that Baylor band. Some of those boys were blowing their bass horns at him. I'd have done the same thing." As we entered Springfield, Illinois, Dean bolted forward and said: "Do you see what I see?"

I followed his gaze, squinting through the windshield, and saw a sight to behold: The Longhorn Motel, decorated with a sizable neon sign in the shape of a longhorn steer, horns and all. "The Lord's with us," Dean said.

The next afternoon we reached Chicago, where we planned to spend another night before going on to South Bend. We needed a hotel for Bevo, and we had come to the right town. After a long search we found a place—a private stall with hay and water that cost $40 for the night. Bevo was in relaxed spirits and caused no trouble. But Dean made a point to admonish the attendant as we left. "Please don't make a mistake now," he said. "This longhorn is the property of the University of Texas. He's too tough for steaks."

Saturday dawned crisp and cloudless, a perfect football day. Bevo, however, was his rambunctious self again. Perhaps he was readying himself for the Fighting Irish. As we drove toward South Bend, he jiggled the station wagon more energetically than ever. Three or four Texas cars spotted us, and there were hee-haws such as you never heard, and "Hook 'em Horns!" reverberating through the autumnal morning.

South Bend was crowded with early arrivals, who gathered around us as we slowly made our way into the parking lot. We put

Bevo on display for two hours before the game, Dean and I taking tuns holding his rope and guarding his hind quarters. There were a few taunts, but mainly the Notre Dame partisans kept a discreet distance, viewing the distinctive visitor with undisguised awe. There was only one disconcerting moment. I had moved away from Bevo's backside long enough to sign an autograph for a Notre Dame student. As I did so, a teenage boy walked right past me. Bevo reared back and kicked, a vicious swipe that might have beheaded the intruder, missing him by inches. "Mercy, don't let that happen again," Dean said. "They'd lynch us on the 50-yard line."

The moment came to lead Bevo in his ceremonial walk around the football field. As we entered from the end-zone gate, I felt the presence of Rockne and the Gipper, and I made sure my unfamiliar 10-gallon hat was perched at just the right angle on my head. Dean also wore a cowboy outfit with new boots, and as we rounded the stadium he lifted his hat and waved it dramatically. It was his finest moment since the Olympics.

We had brought along a stake, and we tied Bevo to it on the grass behind one of the end zones. Momentarily the Texas team gathered nearby to make its entrance, boys I knew from the campus and the dorms, far from home, facing a mighty foe and betraying a little homesick nervousness. "Hey, there's Bevo!" one of them exclaimed as they waited to go on the field. The word spread down the line. "Hot dawg, there's Bevo, with Dean and Willie!" another shouted. "Go get 'em, Bevo!" yelled a hulking lineman with a baby face. As the Notre Dame team made their grand entrance from the far end of the stadium, Charlie Dollar, a Texas halfback, walked up to Bevo and gave him the "Hook 'em" sign.

I remember the unsettling snarls from the Notre Dame offensive linemen, sounded in unison, just before each snap of the ball, and a disastrous interception that led to a Notre Dame touchdown, and Dean Smith's frequent conferences with Bevo when the noise of the crowd made him nervous. I remember, too, the Texan who came down to talk to us at halftime. He had been celebrating. He brought with him an official-size Lone Star flag and introduced himself as a "Texas Ex" from Detroit. "Look here," he said, "we want to make you a swap. We'll give you this flag for Bevo." When we politely refused, he said, "I didn't expect you would anyhow," then, turning to me: "I'll give you this flag for that hat of yours." I thanked him, but declined. "Oh, hell," he said, "then we'll just give you the flag," and staggered away. We put the flag staff in the ground not far from Bevo.

All for naught. Notre Dame could do little wrong that day and beat us, 21–0.

They had to put Bevo out to pasture, and I heard he died sometime after that, and they buried him under some live oaks on the ranch beyond the Balcones. I had long since gone away, but I was a little saddened. In those years of youth, I had thought him too big and ornery to be mortal.

YAZOO CITY HIGH SCHOOL
1950–1952

Photos by Stanley C. Beers

Author Willie Morris was a 17-year-old senior at Yazoo City (Miss.) High School in 1952. He was editor of the school newspaper, *The Flashlight*, and played football, basketball, and baseball.

A "Tom Thumb Wedding" ceremony in 1942 featured (l-r) Willie Morris, groom, Ralph Atkinson, minister, and Vanjon Ward, best man.

Photo by Ralph Atkinson

Willie Morris, 15, perfected his hook shot underneath his backyard goal with schoolmate Pee Wee Baskin.

Disguised as "English lecturer, Sir Whoopin Tom Lipscott, of Catfish-on-the-Muddybank, London," Morris, 16, and his dog Skip entertained his classmates at Yazoo City High.

At band practice in 1951 were (l-r) Jon Abner Reeves, french horn, Jimmy Neeld, baritone, Kenneth Edmondson, bass, and Willie Morris, trumpet.

Flashlight editor Morris interviewed Huntz "Satch" Hall, of Bowery Boys fame, in the lobby of the Dixie Theatre, during the actor's visit to Yazoo City in 1951.

Baseball 1950

Willie Morris (first row, 2nd from left) played center field for the Yazoo City Indians baseball team. The 1950 team (l-r, seated): Atkinson, Morris, McCarley, Coleman, Barrack, H. Wilkinson; (2nd row) Holaday, Coody, C. Wilkinson, Woodruff, Orsborn; (3rd row) Cagle, Shepherd, Fletcher, Cheatham, Johnston, Coach Kelly.

Former Ole Miss basketball star Harold "Hardwood" Kelly, shown with outfielder Red Milner (left) and pitcher Freddie Fletcher, was head basketball and baseball coach and assistant football coach at Yazoo City High.

Photo by Ralph Atkinson

Morris (right) led the 1951 Indians in batting with a .300 average, followed by teammate Red Milner's .262 average. He also won the annual basketball trophy in 1951 for the highest shooting percentage on free throws—82 percent.

Photo by Ralph Atkinson

Morris and friend Ralph Atkinson posed Willie's dog Skip in an all-sports setting in Morris's front yard on Grand Avenue in 1950.

During the 1951 homecoming parade, band director Stanley Beers photographed his Yazoo City band from a second-story window along main street.

The Yazoo City High homecoming queen for 1951 was Daisye Love Rainer.

The majorettes for the 1951 Yazoo City High Marching Band were (l-r) Ina Rae Aven, Kay King, Dee Phillips, Betty Lou Rogers, and Shirley Walne.

The 1951 Indians homecoming court (l-r): Nettie Taylor Livingston, Daisye Rainer, and Kay King.

The 1951 Indians football team was runner-up in the Delta Valley Conference with an 8-3 record, including wins over Kosciusko and Belzoni.

Yazoo City fans overflowed the grandstands at Canton for the 1951 football game on Thanksgiving Day, in the oldest high school football rivalry in Mississippi.

Yazoo City fullback Bobby Rhodes stiff-armed his way past Canton defenders for a 4-yard gain in 1951.

In a night game at Batesville, Tribe benchmen awaited their turn to play.

In 1951 Willie Morris's classmates voted him "Most Versatile, Wittiest, and Most Likely to Succeed."

In the 1951 Who's Who group photo, Morris was second from right, standing.

"Mr. and Miss Yazoo High" for 1951-52 were Charles "Big Boy" Wilkinson and Daisye Love Rainer.

The 1951-52 Yazoo City High basketball team finished 2nd in the Delta Valley Conference (l-r, first row): Rex Nowlin, Muttonhead Shepherd, Bobby Coleman, Willie Morris; (2nd row) Hans Johnson, Bobby Kennedy, Leslie Coody, Robert Pugh, Bubba Barrier; (3rd row) Coach Kelly, Charles Wilkinson, Sanders Powell, Roy Roby, and Edwin Upton, mgr.

Willie Morris played forward on the "starting five" Yazoo City Indians varsity in 1951-52.

Morris (20) scored with a driving layup in the Indians' 34-10 victory over Belzoni in 1952.

Graduation Day for the Class of 1952 in the Yazoo City High gymnasium.

After graduating from Yazoo City High in 1952, Willie Morris headed west for Austin, Texas.

Morris was editor of the *Daily Texan* at the University of Texas and was a Rhodes Scholar at New College, Oxford, from 1956-60.

Willie Morris hit a three-run homer off pitcher Dustin Hoffman to win the 1972 artists-writers' softball game in East Hampton, N.Y., but broke his ankle crossing home plate.

Bringing Basketball to England

To William and Patty Lewis,
Van Dorn Ooms, and Gale Denley

AMERICA WAS doing fine when we went to Oxford in '56, thirty-two Rhodes Scholars in our prime who eyed one another with curiosity during a rough Atlantic crossing on *The Flandre*. The diffidence faded three days out when, after several rounds in the bar, the group went on deck and one by one began climbing a mast. A steward discovered us. "You cannot do that!" he shouted, his Gallic eyes rolling in aversion. "We only send our best men up," replied Ooms, varsity squash, Amherst.

The dollar lasted a long time in those days. The hegemony of the big green passport swept all before it. American SAC bases dotted the English landscape, and the military was everywhere. Brightly-beribboned NATO officers and airmen from Brize Norton and Upper Heyford with their crewcuts walked the High in swarms on weekends and even had their own pubs. I was arrested three times by MP's right there in Oxford in the first month until I learned to let my hair grow.

It was the time of Suez, Budapest, and Adlai Stevenson's second defeat. Eisenhower had eleitis. Dulles spoke of massive retaliation. The fleeting, grey sensual aura of the old town made home seem distant and unreal. Its walls and towers, its spires and cupolas and ancient quadrangles, its fortress aspect as sighted from the river walks when the sun broke through and caught its silhouettes, its bells ringing forever in the rain, gave those early days there a fragile, unearthly ambience. Surely it was the first and last time I would ever live in a museum. New College, my college—and Ooms' of Illinois and Rudenstine's of Connecticut and D'Arms' of New Jersey and Suddarth's of Tennessee—had been new in 1386. We lived in frigid rooms around a copious Victorian quadrangle, surrounded on all sides by Englishmen who used *actually* in every sentence, and mere yards from the Twelfth Century city wall, which traversed the quadrangle and the college gardens beyond. A boys' choir sang madrigals each afternoon from the dark, eerie chapel across the way with Epstein's Lazarus guarding the antechamber and the memorials to the dead of many wars. A giant turtle said to be three hundred years old loitered (what else could it do?) in the shade of the cloisters behind the chapel. We took our meals in a medieval dining hall with its gloomy portraits of warriors and kings, parliamentarians and ecclesiastics. Kipper and oatmeal were for breakfast, vintage roast beef and potatoes for lunch and dinner. The concrete stairs leading to the hall were deeply grooved with the footsteps of the two-score generations. There were always echoes in the fog. The dons were shadowy figures, as terrifying to me as nuns in my childhood. Their table in the dining hall was two feet above the undergraduates, just under the portrait of the Founder, William of Wykeham, with whom they shared a cosmic exemption from mortal languor.

There was an English student there named Lord Willie Nugent, who wore a black cape and pince-nez and carried a cane. He had recently written a book on medieval dungeons. We were told of the morning a year before when a freshly-arrived American approached him, hand extended. "I'm Dick Burdis of Pennsylvania," he said. Lord Willie squinted down, then replied: "Really?" Burdis told us: "I thought he was going to smite me with his cane." Revenge would come at the Christmas party we gave for the Englishmen. Yoder of North Carolina prepared an efficacious Old Catawba eggnog. The English and their women, accustomed to sherry and wine, went berserk in the quadrangle. Some began climbing trees. Others became quietly sick near the old city wall. Lord Willie Nugent approached me, weaving slightly. He had never spoken to me before and, as I recall, never would again. "I say," he asked, "is this what you call a barbeque?"

An expansive leisure lay at the core of the system. A West Point man said he spent most of his first two weeks going to the bulletin boards looking for an order. The weather was morning sunsets, swirling mists, and the unhurried rain. That winter an American of another college, awakened by a friend at seven a.m., exclaimed, "Oh to be in April, now that England's here." There was no requirement to attend lectures, which had been considered obsolete since the invention of the printing press in the mid-Fifteenth Century. The principal compulsion was weekly or twice-weekly essays to be read aloud after prolific research and discussed in private sessions with the dons, and these were formidable exercises that would dispirit the vainest ego. Examinations were comprehensive and came at the end of three years.

The sacrosanct privacy of the place amidst its crumbling walls and forbidding cul-de-sacs elicited a loneliness, a spirit of *angst* and melancholia for this American just emerged from the deltas and cane breaks of Mississippi. It also inculcated in those first weeks the most debilitating lethargy I have ever known. After a year as editor of the student daily at the University of Texas, the change of pace seemed too horrendous for casual adjustment. I began spending considerable time in the pubs with the Australians, a boisterous frontier cadre who blamed the Americans when they got into trouble, which was often. One midnight they purloined a lawnmower and mowed the shaggy carpet in the Senior Common Room. Emerging from the pub one late afternoon into the college, in a diaphanous mist we confronted an eclectic assemblage: elves and fairies and Elizabethan princes and princesses and a girl in white robes playing a flute. "I had too bloody much *this* time," the Aussie from Brewarrina, New South Wales, said, unaware that the college drama club had just finished a Shakespearean rehearsal.

As an inveterate nocturnal prowler, I often thought myself the only living person awake in those hours after midnight when the ghosts of six centuries roamed the corners of the college. A mystic from New Delhi with obscure eyes, also a person of the night, claimed to be in touch with these spirits. I once ran into him in the garden at two a.m., kneeling on the grass, his arms spread toward the heavens in supplication; I got out of there fast. One especially ghoulish night I had the curtains drawn on my windows and was reading Blackstone. A fork fell off a table on the far side of the room. I paid no attention. A few minutes later a pencil rolled off my desk. I looked all around me before escaping again into my book. A short time after that, a photograph of a Mississippi girl drifted to the floor. My heart was pounding as I stood up. In quick succession an ashtray struck the carpet in a far corner, then a spoon, and finally a small box of paper clips. I fetched a knife from my tea cabinet and rushed to the windows, pulling open the curtains, almost collapsing at the sight which greeted me from outside—a white-faced figure, features contorted, garbed in cape and hood. Momentarily this specter began laughing. I recognized D'Arms of New Jersey, caked in talcum powder. He and Ooms had spent all afternoon while I was away tying the objects to long strands of nearly invisible thread; they had been outside pulling the thread.

The West Pointers were the most prosperous people in all of England, drawing the scholarship stipend and full lieutenant's pay and bounteously blessed as they were with the PX privileges of the military bases. They drove sports cars and wore Saville Row suits, dined on steaks and drank Jack Daniel. I began visiting two of the West Point men in their opulent quarters on Banbury Road. Sometimes we played poker and Monopoly. On Saturday nights we drank champagne with American airline stewardesses from London and listened to the college football games on their expensive short-wave radio, the Armed Forces Radio Service doing Notre Dame versus Michigan in Ann Arbor, or Ole Miss versus LSU from Tiger Stadium in Baton Rouge. The roar of the assembled Cajuns in the latter contest reverberated down the hedgerows of North Oxford.

Oh, the drifting, indolent days! Who am I? I would ask myself. What am I doing here? I started going to movies in the darkened early afternoons with a Trotskyite who wore the same maroon pullover every day and refused to wear his false front tooth when he was angry. Occasionally his pale, emaciated girl friend joined us in the little cinema on Walton Street; I wondered if her thinness had to do with the scant rations of the War. After a Grade-B Hollywood movie we would adjourn to the Indian restaurant next door for Madras curry and parathas and beer and meticulously analyze the characters and action of the movie we had just seen, first in Marxian terms, then Freudian, then Christian Existential.

The oppressiveness which inspired these arcane pursuits grew more bewildering, and was compounded by the English girls of Oxford, who were a disappointment. I believe we more or less missed the beauteous, unscholarly girls we had left at home, their sunny countenances. We played touch football in the college quadrangle, attracting groups of the quizzical English. The hoary Warden of the college in his Victorian garb, high gaiters and cape, a historian in vogue at the *fin-de-siecle,* sometimes paused to watch. "Buttonhook!" Suddarth would shout, as the doddering old figure stood there, shaking his great grey head back and forth to the rhythms of the action. One unexpectedly lustrous autumn's noon I retrieved my baseball bat and ball and glove from my trunk and went to get Rudenstine, who was in his rooms writing an essay on Roman Britain, particularly the Romans' fluctuating policy on the construction of Hadrian's northern defenses against the Scots and Picts. Using the Twelfth Century old city wall as an outfield fence, I patrolled it against Rudenstine's flies and drives as my hero Enos "Country" Slaughter had once wandered the outfield barriers for the Cardinals in Sportmans' Park in St. Louis. A bad moment was at hand. Rudenstine hit a long, towering fly. As I retreated to the wall, I watched in apprehension as the ball drifted over it toward the Joshua Reynolds stained-glass windows of the college chapel. I stood in a stricken, icy frieze as the ball missed the glass by inches.

"That's it!" Rudenstine yelled angrily, his face as pallid as mine. He threw down the bat. "That's the last time I'll do *this!*" Then he departed without farewell to his treatise on Roman Britain. I gathered the equipment and returned to my lonesome rooms to write a paper for my philosophy tutorial. The subject before me, as I recall it now from the a quarter of a century's distance, was "What Is Real?"

Eugene Gant's professor (Merton, '04) at Chapel Hill in *Look Homeward, Angel* had boasted that Oxford discourages "the useless enthusiasms." Gazing from the windows of my room across the empty greensward at Lord Willie Nugent perched on a far end of the old wall bird-watching with his binoculars, I wondered in that moment if Oxford might not discourage the *useful* enthusiasms as well. I did not know it then, but a savior was at hand.

The notice on a bulletin board said: "Tryouts for Oxford University Varsity Basketball—Tuesday, October 31, 3 p.m—Cowley Barracks Gymnasium." The words blazed out at me. I had heard about this team, which had made a tour of Poland and Czechoslovakia the previous year. There were only twelve places on the squad, I was told, and several of last year's players were returning. Although basketball was well-established in Europe, and the Soviet monolith had long since turned its bureaucratic attention to Dr. Naismith's invention, it was only a recent arrival to England. The Oxford team played twice a week against the other universities and against emigre teams from the Communist nations in London, finishing every year against Cambridge University. Many of the English seemed to confuse basketball with a polite game called "net ball," played by genteel young ladies in the most proper schools all over England. Never mind. I knew I would turn up at Cowley Barracks out of curiosity, and from old glandular instincts. Given the subtle displacement of my introduction to this mellow spot on the Isis, the contemplation of things well-known from boyhood —jump shots, screens, lay-ups—offered the assurance of familiarity, and perhaps an escape from the malaise.

I was undoubtedly not good enough to make this team, but every Oxford scholar in those days was encouraged to have a "game," for the manly sport if for no other reason, and to exorcise the vapors of the chilling air. My "games" in Mississippi had always been baseball and basketball, pre-eminently the former, and I had served as a fleet centerfielder on state championship teams and on a semipro squad of college players with two future major leaguers on the roster which won the Southern title and finished eleventh in the United States in the national tournament in Wichita, Kansas—a team called the Yazoo City "Screaming Eagles," after a popular tire of that era which Mr. Durwood Teaster, our owner, sold in his tire store. After having suffered a severe back injury in football practice for the Yazoo High Indians, I had played basketball three seasons, usually taped-up like a mummy, with a devastating outside shot and varying degrees of success under backboards. I was six feet one and ran the hundred in ten-flat, and we played in the Delta Valley Conference against other cotton towns—Belzoni, Indianola, West Tallahatchie, Cleveland, Leland, Drew, Batesville, Charleston —and the smaller hamlets of Yazoo County in remote gymnasia where the rural fans hostile to the big-city boys from Yazoo threw lethal objects at us. It was good, if not spectacular high school basketball, and under Coach Hardwood Kelly, a star at Ole Miss in the late 1940's, Bubba Barrier and Muttonhead Shepherd and Big Boy Wilkinson and Bobby Pugh and I—the starting five on a team which came to be known throughout the delta as the "Ten Little Indians"—we received a wholesome grounding in the nuances of the sport.

My thoughts turned to these memories as Ooms, Yoder, and I boarded the double-decker bus on the High that took us to Cowley Barracks, down the industrial streets of an Oxford profoundly removed from the medieval university with its touch of Edwardian England still at hand. I would make that long bus journey many times from one world into another in the wintry afternoon gloom, sometimes taking a history book to evade the sullen prospect. Beyond the Morris Auto Works we came upon Cowley Barracks, an English military base of forlorn exteriors with regimental colors on display in its buildings and a small gymnasium which had been reconverted from a Victorian mess hall. About twenty-five Americans, a Canadian or two, and a Filipino were ready to do drills on the court, which was not quite of regulation length and with wooden backboards more or less ten feet high.

The tryouts and scrimmages lasted several days, and each afternoon we would retire to a pub to talk things over. The names of the returnees were Likens, Dunbeir, Gold, and Sarbanes, and they were an able group of scholar-athletes. Likens, the player-coach,

78

was a seven-foot center who had been captain at the University of North Carolina. Dunbeir and Gold were tall forwards who had performed for Nebraska and City College of New York. Sarbannes, a 6-2 guard, had played at Princeton and was a student of political history, grooming himself there at Cowley Barracks to be United States Congressman and Senator from Maryland.

With these four, the authentic collegiate basketball talent ended. Nonetheless it was to my astonishment that I not only was named to the team—compliments to Hardwood Kelly and the Yazoo High Indians—but was the sixth man, sharing point-guard duties with Schork of Massachusetts. And when Schork hurt his ankle in the third or fourth game, I was in the starting lineup. I returned to my histories and British Constitutional documents with a vigor I thought I had lost forever. The secret lanes and river walks and time-imbued quads and gardens of the magic town assumed an unexpected luster. I even found a girl friend, a pretty English girl at St. Hilda's College from Rye. She had the unlikely nickname "Chicken," a tall blonde with brown eyes and an amiable disposition who helped me forget the double-named girls of the Southland with their gossipy style. We grew to enjoy our interminable hikes through all the majestic colleges with our history guidebooks, and we even shared the ten-pound prize for naming a new pub— "The Scholar Gypsy"—out in the tossing green hills. Only the Warden of Rhodes House dampened this serenity. "What is your game?" he asked during one of our sessions with brandy and cigars. "Basketball," I replied. His brow wrinkled. "But surely, Morris," he said, "isn't that rather like bringing the coal to Newscastle?"

Thus began this brief season of varsity success, satisfying those prepubescent yearnings for athletic grandeur nurtured in a small town of Dixie. Gazing down now from the summit of twenty-five years, I acknowledge I was more likely than not living out a fantasy, though surely not an ignoble one. The ball club was good, and with diligence would have been competitive with the lesser teams of the mightier American conferences.

This team was never so able as the later ones at Oxford, as described to me recently by Josiah Bunting, now the president of Hampden-Sydney College, when the legendary Bill Bradley of Princeton and the New York Knickerbockers was captain of the Oxford squad, and when a succession of fine college basketball players happened to receive the Scholarships and won consistently against the best European and Iron Curtain teams. In one of those later years, the U.S. Air Force All-Star team based in the continental United States came to England to play an important match against the U.S. Air Force All-Stars based in Europe. The American-based players arrived at Upper Heyford three days early. The officer in charge of the team asked the colonel who commanded the SAC base if there might be a basketball team in the area which his squad could play as a warm-up for the European All-Stars. The commandant remembered that the American boys at the University had a team of sorts, and a casual game was arranged. The Yanks from Oxford arrived at the resplendent base gymnasium, each having brought along a book or two. Bill Bradley, I was told, was carrying a copy of Plato's *Republic*. A big Ivy League forward from the University of Pennsylvania had *War and Peace*. Since it was only a warm-up game, they emerged from the dressing room in faded blue Oxford jerseys, scruffed sneakers, and pants that rarely matched. As the American All-Stars drilled in their colorful uniforms down the way, the scholars lackadaisically took their lay-ups and jump shots. "When that game started," Bunting remembered, "I never saw such a surprised crowd." Bill Bradley scored at will, making incredible passes all the while to his teammates. The Air Force players could not fully absorb what was happening to them. After twelve minutes or so, Oxford was ahead 30-8. The rest of the game followed this pattern. When it was over, the Oxford men packed their bags and went back to their books.

There was no such drama for the Oxford Dark Blues of 1956-57, but I wish to believe we were precursors of the grander times, we boys of the Eisenhower years, pioneers on the alien soil, making a tradition much as Rockne had at South Bend, suffering the jibes of the natives about the funny bouncing ball, never failing to be compared unfavorably with rugby, cricket, soccer, crew and even— God forbid—net ball, playing before minuscule crowds, enduring

80

the icy showers of Cowley Barracks, forever explaining the rules of our preposterous game to our bemused English companions. We were, in truth, Dr. Naismith's Johnny Appleseeds.

We scored several early and decisive victories, over teams largely composed of American and European students from the other English universities and the London-based Communist emigre teams, who were awkward, but large and rugged. The unknowledgeable English referees inspired mayhem. I lost a tooth to a flying elbow in a game in London, and although the Polish miscreant apologized in three languages, no foul was called. Near the end of Michelmas term, we were unbeaten in ten games. We journeyed to the out-of-town matches on the British Railway Service, often composing our weekly tutorial essays en route, always drawing clusters of the secretly inquisitive English, who are not a tall breed, because of our size. Likens, at seven feet, and the tall forwards would sometimes walk up and down the aisles of the trains to observe the reactions. The English, discreetly watching this scene, would whisper among themselves. Once I overheard a man who nudged his companion and said, "Do you suppose it's the circus?"

After the games we would return on the trains through the dark miniature land to our City of Dreaming Spires. Late at night and with no one about, we would have to climb the treacherous walls of the locked colleges to get inside. Magdalen and Christ Church and Balliol and Jesus and Oriel and New College were offering no heroes' welcome, for this silent, imposing cloister of lost causes, one surmised, had seen more than basketball come and go. And then, once ensconced in my rooms, nursing my bruises, absorbing the ineluctable silence of the centuries outside my windows, the rustlings of palpable ghosts, the evanescent murmurings of all the vanished young men, the footsteps of the insomniac New Delhi mystic from the quad, and often the laughter of the Australians tottering in mischief on top of the old city wall, I would sit as close to the fire as I could and read the history of England—but nothing beyond 1900. "Anything after that," a comrade from Winchester who knew little of picks, screens, and freezing the ball had warned, "is considered to be journalism."

On weeknights we would sometimes assemble a makeshift team

and go out to play one of the British Army or RAF squads. This opposition, it must be said, did not rank with Indiana or Kentucky. Our English foes were just learning the game. They wore socks that sagged, and their dribbles were neck-high. Occasionally they ran with the ball without bouncing it, and they considered a jump-ball an approximation of the rugby scrum. In the dingy, ill-lit arenas with perhaps four or five dozen people watching, we ran up imposing scores without wishing to. One game ended 106-24, and the spectators kept shouting: *"Shame, Oxford, Shame!"*

One Saturday afternoon we had a game against one such RAF team at 3 p.m. in Cowley Barracks. At lunch that day in the college dining hall, a catastrophic event occurred. The Australians were in a cantankerous mood, having been dipping into what they called the acorn gourd since before breakfast. There was a college tradition, rarely invoked, that if a scholar spoke of a girl he especially admired, or referred in any manner to his present academic work, the student sitting nearest to him might shout the word *"Skowl!"*. Then one of the scouts would bring in a silver medieval tankard of strong beer, half a gallon it seemed, and the offender would be required to consume the entire contents in seconds. The Aussie captain of the Oxford crew, treachery on his mind, claimed he overheard me mention my girl "Chicken." He announced the incantation, and momentarily I was confronted with the monstrous tankard. I dutifully downed that lusty beer. Then the Aussie petitioned the same punishment for previous unreported infractions. Somehow I drank the second tankard.

I staggered down New College Lane with Ooms and Yoder to take the bus to Cowley Barracks. I weaved about the basketball court taking my practice shots. Inexplicably, I could not miss. My spirits were ebullient. Just before the game an American of our acquaintance, a burly Swarthmorian who was the referee that day, came up to me.

"You're in no condition to play," he said. "Go take a cold shower."

"In no *condition?*" I recall my reply. "I'll bet five pounds I score fifty points."

"You're joking."

"No I'm not." Then I hiccoughed.

"You're on, kid."

The match against the hapless RAF men began inauspiciously when I rifled a hard pass to Yoder at the post which hit him on the head and bounded crazily upward toward the rafters. Shortly after that, Ooms dissuaded me from making a fast break toward the enemy end of the court. But then, once the exertion began to clear the blurred images, I could do no wrong. At halftime I had 24 points, and in the second half my teammates began feeding me the ball for lay-ups and hookshots near the basket. "Stop being so persistent," the RAF man who was guarding me said. "I can't help it," I replied. "Please forgive me." I finished with 54 points.

"What brand of ale do you use?" the Swarthmorian inquired as he counted out five one-pound notes. Ooms was standing nearby. I handed him a one-pound note for his deft passes.

The season would continue in Hilary Term after the long Christmas vacation. Several of us spent it in London, taking a suitcase of books down with us. We rented a flat off Bayswater Road, wandering the streets of London in its hermetic fogs, dallying in its splendid museums and galleries and concert halls and bookstores. That Dickensian Christmas tugs even now at my heart—the stores lit brightly in the gloom, the shoppers standing in the bus queues with their parcels, the dressed geese and turkeys hanging in the meatmongerers' windows. "Chicken" arrived from Rye and lightened those December fogs. And there was the House of Commons, where we sat in the Strangers' Gallery mesmerized by the wit and rhetoric of Aneurin Bevan, and where one day an elderly figure strolled in just below and took a seat on a Tory back bench. I could not take my eyes from him. There was a bright red carnation in the lapel of Winston Churchill.

Yet even in such a *milieu*, basketball was not to be denied. Every afternoon we took a bus to the London "Y," a musty, cavernous place, for scrimmages with the Iron Curtain refugees, Spaniards,

Italians, Chinese, and one day a group of students from Ghana who played a brand of basketball patterned more or less after soccer. Sometimes, long after the others had departed, I would remain, for I was perfecting a fadeaway jump-shot from around the key. As in the distant twilights of Mississippi, when I lingered before the basketball goal in my backyard playing a mythical game of my own devising against Tennessee or Kentucky or Vanderbilt, I always sank the winning basket at the buzzer. I was twenty-two years old, in the magnificant old nexus of The Empire at Christmas, but the adolescent had not left me yet.

Shortly after the second term convened in Oxford, we were invited to Boulogne, France, to play the French All-Star team, including several Olympians. The game was to be on a Saturday night; the University granted its permission for an international match, and the French agreed to pay our expenses. We had heard of the French interest in basketball. The government had gone so far as to print postage stamps commemorating the game. We took the boat-train out of London, crossed the Channel, and arrived in Boulogne in mid-afternoon. *"Les gigantesques Americains vont arriver a Boulogne aujord'hui,"* a large headline proclaimed on page one of the newspaper. It was my first trip to Europe, and I was enthralled by its sights and smells on this damp day of January, and I knew I would come back someday for a very long time. I was even more impressed, however, by the gymnasium where we were to play. Reaching it that night in taxis, we found a preliminary game in progress. It was an ancient, barn-like structure, and the stands were crowded with more than two thousand Frenchmen, waving wine bottles and tri-colors. A pale shimmer of Gauloise smoke pervaded this striking scene. On the court itself, boards protruded here and there from the floor, which seemed not quite level but stretched away at a slight list, and a portion of the floor near center-court was covered with a wicked green linoleum. Even with the odor of garlic which hovered about, I was reminded of the little gymnasium in Satartia, Mississippi, on the Saturday nights of my boyhood—the dirt-farmers shouting their taunts, the frizzly-haired women who sat there prim and embarrassed, the over-charged atmosphere of boondocks hostility, the smell of bodies too warm and close together.

We were using what was then known as the "European ball" that night—a basketball the size of a volleyball. As we ran onto the court to the cries of incredulity at the size of Likens, Dunbeir, and Gold—Likens was dunking during the warm-ups, and every time he did so a primal gasp rose from the stands, and the chatter of foreign tongues—I sensed we were in trouble. It was not so much the French Olympians, who were fast and adroit and obviously versed in the fundamentals, although their tallest man was no more than 6'6". It was the ball itself. I discovered right away that shooting a volleyball is not like shooting a basketball. A volleyball is not merely smaller, of course, but livelier and more erratic, with a mind of its own. In the warm-ups, we found ourselves time and again shooting what later became known on American television as "air balls"— shots which never reached the rim or even the backboard. Down the court I noticed the Frenchmen were comfortable with their minuscule ball; they rarely missed.

After *The Marseilles,* this advantage became apparent. To the roar of their followers, the French took a swift, commanding lead. Likens' height under the basket was negated by their deadly accuracy and their clever plays. They were very good, and the officiating was plainly in their favor. Our shots continued to fall far short of their mark. Only Sarbanes, who grew accurate with the curious little ball, and Likens, who began relying on ingenious Carolina tactics under the goals, prevented an early annihilation. But at the half we trailed by sixteen points.

In the dressing room, an ominous chamber with a wet concrete floor, we slumped in our seats. Sarbanes broke the silence. "We're supposed to be smart," he said. "Let's use our heads. For one thing, I found out you have to shoot the volleyball about two feet longer than you think you want to." Likens added that he intended to begin lobbing long passes downcourt as soon as he got a rebound. "Somebody be there," he said. Then he diagrammed three or four plays to take advantage of a weak defensive forward.

As the second half began, the tide of that game slowly turned. Fast breaks with Likens' lobs were working. Using their elbows, our forwards began to make easy lay-ups. Following Sarbanes' advice, I began shooting the volleyball farther and sank three or four jumpshots from the outside. On instinct, I broke toward our basket just before we had rebounded and got a simple lay-up, but the next time I tried it I was knocked into a row of chairs, landing on the lap of a hefty French matron. *"Pardonnez-moi, madame,"* I remember saying, but no foul was called. We were edging closer as the minutes went by. Then disaster struck when both Likens and Gold fouled out. The French played a delaying game in the final minutes, and we drew even more fouls. With two seconds left, I flung a baseball-like desperation shot from the center of the court which sailed far over the backboard. We lost, 69-68. The spectators sang a spontaneous *Marseilles*. As we shook hands with the happy French players, the crowd came onto the floor and asked for autographs. A little girl approached me:

"I study English in the school. Please write your name in the book."

"Of course I will, honey."

"Now, please, a lock of the hair." She withdrew a small pair of scissors and motioned for me to lean down.

As we left the dressing room, outside in the chilly night air with mists from the Channel, a throng of the French awaited us. They were working-class men and women, roughly dressed, and they passed around bottles of *vin rouge* and shouted *"Vive l'Amerique!"* We signed more autographs. From far in the distance came the echo of a boat's horn. A Frenchman produced an accordian, and we lingered there with the crowd a few minutes longer. Then we departed for our pension.

"That was fun," I said to Sarbanes.

He agreed. "But wouldn't you like to get 'em at home in Mississippi on Saturday night with a regulation basketball?"

The season continued through February into March, our only loss being to the French. In the midst of the regular varsity schedule, New College upset Christ Church in the finals of the All-College Tournament at Cowley Barracks, as Ooms sank thirty points. It proved to be the only college athletic championship won by New College all that year of 1956-57, but no one seemed to know. We dedicated this victory to the memory of the Founder, William of Wykeham, but he looked down on us from his portrait as grim-visaged as ever. The only person who watched this final match was an Englishman of our acquaintance from Plymouth, who for reasons inexplicable to me kept running along the edge of the court yelling: *"Up, College!"*

As the winter gradually softened, the time came for the national tournament in London, an invitational bringing together the four best teams in England. We defeated a team of Polish refugees by ten points in a well-appointed gymnasium and then, the next night, before some 1,500 spectators, in our most flawless game to date, crushed the British National Team, the equivalent of their Olympians, by twenty-five.

We retired to a pub near Paddington Station to celebrate our national championship, then boarded the train to Oxford. Once more Ooms and I had to climb into the college after curfew. The only way to accomplish this was to scale a ten-foot wall which loomed before us down an ephemeral walkway. From experience we knew the crevices and outcroppings in the ancient brick, which offered precarious places for our feet. Once on top of the wall, avoiding the shards of glass embedded there, we knew also that three careful movements of the legs would get us over the long, sharp spikes to our foothold on the other side before the last jump to earth. This tripartite movement over the spikes was the most dangerous part of the exercise; Palmer of Kettering still had a nasty scar on his back from having taken the spikes too gingerly. On this wet, windy night my companion and I panicked, just as we had the first few times we had tried to scale this barrier. We were tired, and we could not muster the courage to make the grotesque pirouettes that would carry us to safety. We crouched there in the drizzle for a long time.

"Hell," Ooms finally said. "If we'd won the national championship back home, all the girls would've been at the station. The band would've been there, too. Just look at us now."

In our dressing room after the championship game in London, a lieutenant-colonel in the American Air Force had come in and introduced himself. "Congratulations, men," he said breezily. Then he extended us an invitation to play his team at Brize-Norton, a SAC base thirty miles in the countryside from Oxford. After the game we would be guests in the Officers' Club for drinks and dinner, the colonel said. We could also buy some items in the PX if we wished. We agreed on a match one afternoon the following week.

The Air Force dispatched a bus for us. When we entered the gigantic base, we were in another world entirely—the America of the late 1950's: trim houses with mothers in hair-curlers tending their children, Buicks and Chevrolets, a baseball diamond, gum-chewing airmen with scuttle-shaped chins tossing footballs, voices from the mountains and ghettos and swampbogs and prairies, all of this suffused with an affluence we had nearly forgotten. Immense silver airships sat far out on the runways, guarded by figures wearing holsters. The PX was our first stop. We entered the glass doors past a tough-looking sergeant who eyed us warily until the colonel explained our mission. Inside we were greeted by recorded popular tunes. Air Force wives in slacks and sneakers with children roamed among the booze and groceries, the pyramidal stacks of chicken-a-la-king, Hormel chili, Uncle Ben's Rice, Macadamia nuts, and kleenex. One huge set of counters was filled with children's toys of every description, another with cameras and Kodachrome film, and the frozen-food section was large as a warehouse. I bought a quart of Cutty Sark and some baseball bubble-gum cards.

We played in a shiny new gymnasium with three or four hundred people from the base there to watch, including what must have been a whole classroom of American children. The referees were the best we had seen all year, but we were sloppy in the first half. The team we were playing was half white and half black, big and fast. But we kept a steady lead, and pulled away to win by twelve points. After the game, in the Officers' Club, we luxuriated in the steaks and martinis, and watched the shapely officers' wives with yearning, and listened to Frankie Laine and Johnny Ray and Nat (King) Cole on the juke-box. The same colonel came over to our table. "Men," he said, "you just defeated our base intra-mural champions. Would you care to play our varsity next Friday?"

We came out again under the same circumstances. In the PX, I purchased at the toy-counter a sinister game of wits called Southwest Conference Football. This time there was a larger crowd, and more vociferous support for the home team. They did not need it. They consisted of ten blacks, including a 6'10" center, two 6'8" forwards, and a lightning-quick guard, from Brooklyn I learned, who was better than any college guard I had seen. None of them, we were told later, had ever been to college. They were as adept as a strong college team, aggressive and well-coached. They won by twenty points.

The landscape was poised now between winter and spring. The term was coming to an end, and so was our season. We received a formal invitation from the Soviet government to represent England in the Moscow Games that summer. The Soviets would pay our way to Berlin, and fly us from there to Moscow on a special plane. An exhibition tour of the Russian provinces was suggested. But *realpolitik* intervened. The State Department and the Foreign Office advised us it was not in the "best interests" of the United States or Great Britain for us to go. It was the height of the Cold War; not until the Porgy and Bess troupe two years later would there be a significant cultural exchange. We protested. It was our responsibility as scholars to see Russia. Finally, the venerable university itself refused to let us go.

We had one last game that year, the traditional rivalry against Cambridge University. Anyone who played in this game would receive a "half-blue," the equivalent of a varsity letter. Rather than a monogrammed "O," however, the "half-blue" was a dark blue-and-white tie, emblem of the Oxford athletic teams.

I came across my "half-blue" tie not too long ago as I was moving out of a house on eastern Long Island. There is was, in one of several boxes containing the mementos of those years, the debris and paraphernalia of my own Oxford—old tutorial essays written in a young man's prose that stalks me now like the beastly predator, the menu of a Commemoration Ball, the tassle from my mortar board, a scroll the Aussies had given me making me an honorary Australian, a lecture schedule for Michelmas Term of 1956, yellowed invitations to sherries and teas, my Oxford diploma, faded photographs catching the revelry of a golden April afternoon, the group picture of all of us on the deck of *The Flandre* looking so indisputably American and ready for the world, the baseball that almost broke the stained-glass windows, a few letters from my English girl—where are you now, my dear "Chicken"? The old blue-and-white tie was worn and mildewed, the blue nearly faded away, the white a sickly grey. With a ceremonious gesture, I threw it into the garbage. But it made me remember the Cambridge game.

Cambridge was a home match for us at Cowley Barracks and I had brought "Chicken" along with me, for she had never been to one of our games. The familiar old gymnasium was festive that day. The English soldiers had polished it so that it gleamed as it never had before; an Oxford-Cambridge match, even if in basketball, was not to be taken lightly, for it had the magnitude of history behind it. The Oxford-Cambridge rugby match might draw 80,000 people at Twickenham, and the Boat Race was a national event like the World Series, as was the cricket match at Lords, but who would deny the intrinsic attraction of an Oxford-Cambridge basketball game? Some of the English girls had draped the bleachers in the dark blue crepe of Oxford, and the light-blue of Cambridge, and a capacity crowd turned out that Saturday afternoon from both universities, both English and Americans and their girls, all dressed for the party that would take place afterwards. The Aussies were there to cheer us on, and even one of my history dons, who accepted the invitation in the spirit of inquiry. The Cambridge players were, of course, Americans also, and there was a camaraderie about mutual friends and mutual universities and the news from home. Then the game got down in earnest.

I did not know it that day, but this would be my last real game of basketball. The following winter, in practice just before the season, I would break my hand in three places, and before it could mend I had to go home for a long time because of my father's terminal illness. There was no premonition of my farewell to basketball that day —or was there? Had not the catcher in *Bang the Drum Slowly* gotten better the closer he came to death? I remember my high school coach, Hardwood Kelly, telling us before the important games —"Hang loose as a goose." I pretended that Cambridge University was Belzoni, Mississippi, High School, and that the agile opponent from Indiana who was one-on-one with me was the wily Belzoni guard of those delta days, "Lightnin" Boult. I felt fine and free, sinking the jumpers I had practiced in the London "Y," and we played a team game that was a monument to that uncommon, long-ago year, bringing it all together for the memory of it— perfect screens, deadly passes, uncanny accuracy. The dark Blue won decisively, and the mood in the dressing room was mellow and satisfactory.

"Chicken" was waiting for me outside in the sunshine with some of our friends. She was wearing a blue and white dress and a wide-brimmed dark blue hat. She kissed me on the cheek. "I didn't understand a thing in there," she said, "but I'm rather proud of you for putting that roundball in that hole."

One For
My Daddy

*To Cornelia and Cap—and Squirrel
Griffing, Ed Morgan, Ron Hoka, and Dees*

I WENT up to revisit my friends on eastern Long Island not too long ago. I had lived there for several years before moving on home. I still held my village, Bridgehampton, in the most affectionate regard, for it is enveloped by one of the most beautiful terrains in America—the dark flat earth, the serene ponds and inlets, the sand dunes, the ocean.

Two things saddened me on this return, each having much to do with the passing of time. First, I was without my dog Pete, my beloved Black Lab who had been the unofficial mayor of the town. Pete had moved in with me when he was two years old, in about 1973, and we grew so inseparable that he eventually departed with me to live in Mississippi. He died of old age in Oxford only three months before my visit to Bridgehampton, so that now as I strolled the cherished lanes of the village I expected him at any moment to appear around the corner before me, or to emerge from the shrubs and bushes by the church or the graveyard and tenderly greet me as he always had. Pete was not there.

The second disquieting recognition involved the changes there. The umbilical relationship with the worst aspects of New York City, only one hundred miles to the west, had deepened in my years away. The chic food shops and boutiques had quadrupled. There were more shrinks and gynecologists in their BMW's than ever. It was summertime, and people moved about in packs. The neighborhood seemed taken over, irrevocably and forever, by a careless and deracinated species of modern Americans I had come to call "groovies," who always descend with their money on the old and settled American places.

It was not always so. We had a quieter village life there once. The writers and artists mingled freely with the "locals." We had our own bars and restaurants and hideaways, our beach cookouts at twilight and our spur-of-the-moment excursions to Shelter Island or the North Fork. We even had our own softball team.

It was a good team, too. We called ourselves the Bridgehampton Golden Nematodes, after the insects which attacked the young potato plants without succour or mercy. I was the manager and first baseman, the position the older souls invariably move to in the declining years. The Nematodes were composed of bartenders, potato farmers, teen-agers, a couple of auto mechanics and high school coaches, and two or three writers—a team of unusual ethnic diversity held together by Jeffersonian democracy and the double-steal. Billy DePetris, our ace pitcher, owned the Triple Crown Saloon and Restaurant on the main street. He had played high school baseball with Carl Yazstremski, and he had the most efficacious knuckle-ball in the neighborhood. We played teams from all over the Island on the field behind the Bridgehampton high school where the young Yaz had once hit his memorable drives, and we often drew crowds of two or three hundred people who might bring their picnics and sit on the soft green grass around the diamond. Our players were the DePetris Brothers and Hearst and Calabrese, Shaw and Jones and Rana, Lambrecht and O'Brien and the Morrises (father and son). Twice a year we played a team from Brooklyn called the Titanic Shipping Corporation, who journeyed out with their wives and girl friends and filled the air with the cadences of Flatbush. We always played on languid Sunday afternoons; sometimes, when there was a lull in the activity, one might hear the roar of the ocean from the distance, and the echo of the gulls.

The Nematodes had two owners, who bought the balls, bats, and uniforms. One was Jack Whitaker, the legendary sports television commentator who owned a house near the beach. The other was a formidable entrepreneur named Otis Glazebrook who managed the foam insulation company, so that on our jerseys in script letters were: "Whitaker-Glazebrook Sports." Whitaker had long since retired from active softball, and when he was at home from his assignments at the Kentucky Derby or the PGA tour he watched our games from behind home plate with a certain bemused detachment. Because the other owner, however, believed he could play (on this he was mistaken), I would have to insert him into the outfield in the late innings of games in which we held commanding leads. I continued to do so until the afternoon he circled dubiously under a tall fly ball, which proceeded to hit him on the head, knocking him out cold.

We won the championship of eastern Long Island in one of those latter summers, having challenged the Number One team in the regular league. They were a tough cadre of locals, young and in shape, and they laughed at the prospect, we were told, of playing our eclectic Bridgehampton squad. Five hundred fans were in attendance that Sunday as a benefit for the Animal Shelter, as well as my dog Pete, who twice stopped the action by visiting with me on the field. This historic match was, in truth, decided in the first inning. Leading off for the Golden Nematodes, centerfielder David "Speed" Morris swung on the first pitch and drove it barely fair down the left field line; he slid safely into third in a cloud of petulant dust. Shortstop Cal Calabrese brought him home with a double, and leftfielder Joe Luppi sent Calabrese around with a clothesline single. That was it. Billy DePetris' knuckler was incomparable on this azure summer's day, and the Nematodes took the championship, 2-0. The tough team of locals did not show their faces during the fall and winter.

It was not so much this Homeric victory which remains in my memory, however, as the celebration at Billy's Triple Crown afterwards—the frosty mugs of beer, the triumphant exultings, and then the moment we rose solemnly at the bar and played the song from the jukebox, singing along with Rudy Valee *The Whiffenpoofs' Song*.

It was later that summer, there on the eastern tip of Long Island, that I played my last serious game. I recall it now as vividly as I do my departure from basketball in the Oxford-Cambridge match of 1958. That final game must inevitably be recorded here for its qualities of poetic retribution.

Every August for many years the writers who lived in the Hamptons had played the artists and actors in a benefit softball game. The twenty-fifth renewal of this event was to take place on the diamond in East Hampton. It was a fund-raiser, if memory correctly serves me, for George McGovern's Presidential campaign, which in itself may have suggested something of doom. A capacity crowd, some three thousand people, was assured for this impassioned event, which the writers had won twenty-five years in a row.

And they were all there on this luminous afternoon—the heirs and heiresses to the great Eastern wealth, the movie starlets and owners of the Manhattan art galleries, the New York book editors and publishers, plus dozens of writer and artist groupies and a generous representation of the indigenous Long Island locals, including the faithful Nematodes. Our squad was stocked with deft but aging writers who had athletic pasts—George Plimpton, Joseph Heller, Peter Matthiessen, Peter Maas, Harry Minitree to name a few, as well as Senator Eugene McCarthy, a former minor league player who always came from Washington to participate in these games. He qualified to perform for the writers because he had once published a volume of verse. (In a close play at home plate that day, McCarthy ran over the enemy catcher to score a run, and later observed to me on the bench: "And the Democrats say I'm not *mean* enough.") The artists and actors were not only younger but were consumed with the mood of revenge. After twenty-five years of failure, who could not vouchsafe them that?

The game moved along closely for several innings. The opposition seemed to sense something epic in the making. So did the galleries; the onlookers were so suffused with the summer Hamptons *ennui* that most of them obviously hoped for an end to the writers' victory skein. From my post at first base, out of deferences to the past, I made a number of good fielding plays, but at the plate I had popped up weakly three times and was keenly embarrassed.

Then, quick as could be, with the score tied 5-5 in the top of the ninth inning, the artists-actors erupted for two runs, and going into the bottom of the ninth led 7-5. Their wives and girl friends standing along the baselines among the holiday throng laughed and made exuberant pirouettes, and even the man on the loudspeaker seemed on their side.

As the final inning was about to begin, the spirits on the writers' bench were despondent. "Come on, chaps!" George Plimpton shouted in an effort of false cheer. "What would Tolstoi and Balzac think?"

Dustin Hoffman was on the mound for the artists-actors, an agile young man whom I suspected was throwing a Hollywood spitter. He had come in during the seventh inning and had set our side down in order ever since.

A feeling of imminent drama descended on the crowd as Dustin Hoffman induced Joe Heller to ground out second to first and Peter Matthiessen to pop up to short right field. There were two outs and we were behind by two runs. But it was not over yet. Eugene McCarthy lined a single to center. Plimpton moved now to the plate.

I crouched with two bats in the on-deck circle as Plimpton took a called strike on the corner, then tamely fouled a Hoffman spitter into the dirt. I surveyed the scene before me. Dust rose from the infield, and there was the smell of resin and freshly-cut grass. How often had I waited tensely in the on-deck circles of my youth to challenge a mean son-of-the-earth on the pitcher's mound! How many times in the faraway Mississippi summers of boyhood had I contributed to a close victory! I recalled now the year we won the state championship, the Delta belles in the grandstand, the wicked curveballs of Seth Morehead of Louisiana.

Awash now in these memories, I watched as the indomitable Plimpton singled to left. We had runners on first and second with two out.

As I walked to the plate, I was overcome by yet another memory— of my father batting flies to me behind the armory in Yazoo, of him and the American Legionnaires sitting behind first base conferring on strategy, of those wasted hopes he once had that I might become a great ballplayer. He had been gone now all these years—buried under a mimosa on the last hill before the Mississippi Delta. As I stood in at the plate against Hoffman I could almost hear him calling out to me.

Hoffman turned his back to doctor the ball. Then he peered down at me.

I whispered to myself: This one is for my daddy.

The pitch came in at a fast angle. I timed myself for its treacherous mucilagenous drop, then swung with the strength and yearning of old times past. The crack of the bat resounded across the field. McCarthy and Plimpton began to move as the ball lifted in a mighty arc toward left-center. As I rounded first it was still going, and I watched as it rose higher and higher and disappeared over the mesh fence abutting the tennis courts.

I turned at third and crossed home plate. I tripped over a pothole there. I felt something snap in my foot, and a searing pain.

I sat in the grass as my teammates congratulated me. We had won, 8-7. "Good hit, man," Dustin Hoffman said.

The ankle swelled monstrously in the night. The next morning *The New York Daily News* had a photograph of me crossing the plate, my foot at the most grotesque angle. Someone took me to Dr. Spinzia in Southampton. I reclined in his office as he examined the photograph with a magnifying glass.

"I've been practicing bone medicine twenty years," he said. "This is the first time a patient brought in a picture of a bone actually breaking. Was it worth it?"

I did not need to answer.

The Search for
Billy Goat Hill

*To Ed Perry
and His Worship, John Leslie—
and, of course, to David.*

I TOOK the same route of my college days, when I drove the long stretch from my Mississippi delta town to Austin in a vintage black-and-white Plymouth with dual exhausts. It was a demanding drive then, and it is now, but off the Interstate at Shreveport and southwest on Highway 79, the little towns of East Texas have hardly changed at all. I remember driving through this terrain at the Christmas times of my boyhood, the capacious Texas skies and the holiday decorations along the wide, forlorn streets, and the buoyant happiness of homecoming. Distant expanses of fields, weathered courthouses, lazy intersections I once knew, greet me now in the most haphazard *deja vu*. Carthage, Palestine, Buffalo, Franklin, Herne, Rockdale, Thrall—have they existed in a dreamy hush all these years, and awakened now just for me?

My companion is a good friend from Oxford, the chairman of the appropriations committee of the Mississippi House of Representatives, a high spirited figure of gentle temper in his late thirties, whose admirers claim him to be the third most powerful man in the whole sovereign state of Mississippi. He was chosen to accompany me on this journey to visit my son David, because he has never been to Austin and because, as the money man in the legislature of America's poorest state, he says he wishes to view at close range the fabled oil and gas wealth of the University of Texas.

Euphorically driving deeper into Texas, I tell him of the first time I came this way, a frightened seventeen-year-old in a Greyhound fresh out of Yazoo City, Mississippi, about to enroll in the University. My father, who never went to college, had heard it was the finest university in the South, and in the spring of my senior year he went there to investigate, returning with an enthusiastic report. Bubba Barrier and I ran into him before a baseball tournament on the day he returned to Jackson, Mississippi, playing poker in Firehouse No. 3. They had a main building thirty stores high with a Greek temple on top, he said, a student newspaper which was published every day compared with the *Yazoo Hrald* which came out only once a week, and the most impressive baseball field he had ever seen. Nevertheless, as I crossed the Mississippi River at Vicksburg on that faraway leave-taking, I could not envision what awaited me at the end of Route 79. I did not know a single person in Austin, Texas. Recalling that solitary adventure evoked in a rush for me now the loneliness and fear and the homesickness so dreadful that my heart literally palpitated with pain.

In describing this to my friend, the Mississippi chairman, I started adding the years and was struck with an awesome recognition— twenty five years ago to this very weekend, *a quarter of a century,* I had graduated from the University of Texas. After four years of study in England, I had returned to edit *The Texas Observer* in the early 1960's, but I had only come back to Austin once since 1962, and that was on the briefest of visits. The Austin of my day was still a rather somnolent capitol-and-university town, a fragile blend of the South and the West, with handsome boulevards and immense old houses that always seemed to brood upon some tragic secret, and everything encompassed in a territory of surpassing loveliness. All this had the feel for me of another small Southern capitol town —Jackson—where I spent the summers of my childhood. The sad, graceful hills to the west, which some thought was where the South itself ended and the West began, had inspired O. Hnry to call Austin "The City of the Violet Crown." I subsequently grew to love that town and that campus, for they educated me and allowed me to grow up, suffering me through my Wolfean prose, touching me with a spirit of freedom and possibility—my fustian days. The University, only a few blocks from the splendid pink-granite Capitol, had 15,000 students, which was more than enough for a boy from a Mississippi town with half that many people; yet once one became immersed in it, the University was far from forbidding, but was rather like a middle-sized town suffused at once with languor and ambition. Now friends told me Austin had grown into a metropolis of 300,000, and that the University itself had expanded to almost 50,000. Austin had become something of a crosswords for the East and West Coasts, and young people all over the nation had been advised, in roughly such words: "Enjoy the Sun Belt. Go to Austin." Yet it had pleased me that my son David, just turned twenty-one and choosing to spend several months in Austin between his junior and senior years in college in the East, had fallen in love with this community just as I had those many years ago. I supposed there was an appropriate continuity in that for me.

We had been twelve hours out of Mississippi when the familiar skein of Highway 79 gave way to the new interstate a few miles north of Austin at Round Rock, which once had been a nondescript town whose principal industry was an orphanage but now had all the appurtenances of a breathless suburb. It was that moment before the twilight, and momentarily, out of old instincts, I found myself straining to catch the first glimpse of the University Tower and the dome of the Capitol awash in the sunset, just as I had searched the horizon for these formidable eminences time without number in my youthful comings and goings. Something was wrong, however, for they were nowhere to be found. I thought the new interstate had caused my disorientation, so that I began examining the opposite side of the artery in considerable desperation. Then I realized that the city had expanded outward so catastrophically—a sea of vast twinkling lights in the distance and mile upon mile of motels and franchise establishments—that the ascertainable landmarks were much further down the road. Austin seemed to have overflowed on every side into an irridescent estuary. Finally, after a maze of upper and lower levels transsecting the interminable new buildings, I sighted my honored silhouettes against the orange horizon.

My visit to this disparate Austin helped me know what Mark Twain meant when he returned after many years to Hannibal: "I had a sort of realizing sense of what the Bastille prisoners must have felt when they used to come out and look upon Paris after years of captivity and note how curiously the familiar and the strange were mixed together before them." Surely every generation of us tacitly expects the physical lineaments of its given moment on earth to remain forever as they were in the heart's core, even when knowing this cannot be so. Certainly not in a society which destroys and reshapes with such schizophrenic ardor, and especially in a portion of that society—the American Southwest— where formless destruction had for years amounted to a kind of anthropological imperative. There is no reason to be self-righteous in one's disappointments, yet this yearning for some palpable touch with the physical past is deep and primal, perhaps even among the destroyers, for the human species is distressed enough by any measure on its mysterious cinder of a planet, and this hope that known things might endure a little longer is a wish of the blood, a cry for belonging and assurance in the greater darkness. Most Americans of recent generations have experienced in anguish the transmutations of their past, forgetting the words of the Preacher in *Ecclesiastes,* when he reminds us that only a few things lasteth at all. Yet the injunctions of the Preacher, old as time, do not assuage the pain—especially not for me as I wandered among the approximate scenes of my college years as if in a dream, with the shadowy admonition of the dreamer that he may, perhaps, have been here before.

We dined that night in what had been my favorite Mexican restaurant, but no sooner had I walked inside than I knew it was not my favorite Mexican restaurant at all. Only the name remained. The cool, private spot with the understated below-the-border decor where we once consumed the icy mugs of beer and the incomparable chicken enchilladas and tested our Spanish on the benignly patient waiters had given way to a sort of warehouse, Tex-Mex Kafka, noisy, crowded, and antiseptic. What had become of my cherished place? Had I ever really been there? This awareness of briskness, of bustling and impersonal crowds, grew more acute in my subsequent peregrinations into my past—heavy traffic on

"The Drag," which is the University's main street; a whole terrain of old houses and streets ripped raw between the campus and the Capital for parking lots, parking garages, and garish government buildings; packed restàurants; all the ambiance of a metropolis sprung full-born.

The next day, a hot, bright Texas afternoon, my son David, my friend the Chairman of Mississippi finances, and I set out on a long walk around campus. I had been looking forward to this, for I have forever been haunted, obsessed even, by coming back to known places, by absorbing the precise textures of vanished moments, as if the simple act of the wanderer's reappearance would postpone the tide of mortality. This was not to be. Many of the somewhat dejected establishments of my memory of The Drag itself were replaced now by the kinds of shops which always arrive with growth and money, as Martha's Vineyard or eastern Long Island, *arrivistes* of mod-chic named Jack in the Box and Krazy Korner. The rather disreputable frame building a block off The Drag on Twenty-fourth Street which had housed *The Texas Observer,* that maverick political and literary journal, where I had often worked all night while combatting the roaches, had been transformed into a headquarters for several svelte shops: Easy Rollers, The Body Shoppe, The Ultimate Shop. With trepidation I led my companions into this sacred fount of hard, immemorial labors. The actual quarters for our journal, a long room with a precarious floor, was now an enterprise called The Inner Sanctum, with a sign on the door which said: "No Food, Drinks, or Skates." Back outside, the parking lot was now a sidewalk cafe of glittering aspect named Les Amis, where I sighted a student reading *The Village Voice.* And across the street, where Ronnie Dugger and Sarah Payne and I had habitually repaired in the midst of our deadlines for strong coffee and greasy hamburgers in an all-night eatery out of Edward Hopper, what had we here? A fashionable high-rise, twenty stories tall! Indeed, the more I looked the more of these high-rises sprang from nowhere, gaunt intruders in all directions, mocking me direly in my spirits.

We ascended to the campus proper, up The Mall past the block-long Student Union toward the Tower, where the mad sniper with the tumor on his brain had wreaked bloodshed and murder years before. They do not allow visitors to the observation deck there now; it is eerie and silent as I gaze upward. Farther down the stone is the inscription which titillated me as a youngster: "Ye Shall Know the Truth and the Truth Shall Make You Free." My memories of this campus with its fine Spanish architecture and its soft open spaces is somehow affixed on a languid spring afternoon, students reclining in the shade reading Hemingway, the athletes with *UTAA* on their T-shirts perched on the concrete bannisters near the statue of Woodrow Wilson watching the coeds walk by, a three-legged dog named Tripod who was the campus mascot trailing his favorite students into class, the Capitol in the distance beyond the Fountain and the serene boulevards, the pristine vanity of youth in a beautiful and opulent setting.

But now the empty greenswards of my past were filled to bursting with tall new buildings, as if they had been crammed there as afterthoughts, giving to these grounds the aura of a cocksure technocratic society, an organized milieu which sweeps all before it. Soon, to the east of the Tower, I became lost. Was this the university where I had spent the most ebullient years of my existence, or had I been tricked, set bodily in the middle of UCLA, or Ohio State, or the University of Illinois at Champagne-Urbana? I groped for esteemed and familiar fixtures. Then the old Geology Building appeared before me, and I recognized the words inscribed on the stone, ironic now: "O Earth, What Changes Hath Thou Seen." The Chairman of the Mississippi Appropriations Committee and my son were following a few paces behind me. The Chairman was in awe of these heady surroundings. "Money," he kept muttering. *"Money, money, money!"* As for myself, I silently asked the plaintive query: Why, Texas, did you let it get so big so quickly? . . . and I remembered then the quizzical speech I had once heard given by the Queen of England when I was at Oxford University: "The past is no longer with us, the present is here today, and the future is yet to be."

Now, as we moved downhill on the campus, there was the old

Gregory Gymnasium, and we tarried inside, in the imperturbable empty corridors, looking in the display windows at the trophies honoring the bygone mayhem and glory of the Longhorns. In the tiny office down the hall I had stopped on my way to class most days to see Bibb Falk, the Longhorn baseball coach, who had played twenty years in the major leagues and who would sit there reading *The Sporting News* and talking to me from his interminable store of baseball genius. A few paces farther inside was the Longhorn basketball court, long since abandoned for a superlative palace called the Super-Drum. Outside again, my pulse quickened, for I sensed I was approaching the most familiar domain of all. Around the corner somewhere would be the Men's Tri-Dorms, adjacent to the singularly impressive intramural field which had stretched away for half a mile or more toward the Capitol. Across from the dorms and the field would be the row of establishments we had called "The Slum Area"—a couple of dubious beer parlors, a pool hall, a row of ramshackle student residences and the inestimable Snak Shak where we came at midnight for coffee and apple pie to dally with the waitresses. But as I turned this corner, I saw The Slum Area had vanished forever from the face of the earth, as had the athletic fields, displaced by the ubiquitous hybrid modern structures which seemed approximately two months old. One in particular was prominent. "Oh, my God," I caught myself saying. "What have we *here?*" It was a library shaped like the State of Texas.

By now, in the broiling afternoon heat, David and the Mississippi Chairman were beginning to enjoy my reactions. "How many students did you say are enrolled here?" the Chairman asked.

"Fifty thousand," I said.

"This school has more people than the second largest city in Mississippi," he said.

Once again I was disarranged. Where was Breckenridge Hall? I had spent three years there, on the fourth floor of that raw, unkempt hostelry in a room overlooking the intramural fields, walking to it across the muted campus at night after having filed my *Daily Texan* stories to remain awake laden with No-Doz until dawn studying my books, gazing from my windows every so often at the raucous swarms of students in The Slum Area. Down on the third floor, the baseball players dwelled in their miserable squalor. *"Chicken Ranch!"* they would shout on late weekend afternoons, the words echoing down the hallways, enjoining others to make the drive to that house of ill-repute in La Grange sixty miles away (that fabled institution which my *Harper's* partner Larry L. King would later make famous as the best little whorehouse in Texas). One Saturday before a football game they took the emergency fire hoses and washed down the Baylor University marching band. They roamed the darkened campus at all hours, once locating the underground mechanism which controlled the clock on top of the Tower, so that the chimes sometimes sounded eighteen, or twenty-two. They periodically held auctions in a empty room on the third floor, which was so befouled that the occupants had moved out of it and slept on cots in the hall, and sold water-logged baseballs, cheat notes, mildewed athletic socks, dog-eared textbooks, and once a pair of second-hand water wings. Surely they had not torn down Breckenridge Hall.

And soon, there it was, just as it had always been, but it seemed grotesque and bereft now, with new edifices on all sides of it, an impoverished dwarf, a sad anachronism among all the affluent additions. Where the splendid intramural fields had once been stood a monstrous new dormitory with a medieval motif, turrets and all, which appeared before me as large as the Pentagon. Old B-Hall greeted me and tugged at my soul. It had become a claustrophobic enclave. On this terrace we would sit after having had dinner in the ramshackle wooden cafeteria also long ago vanished and wave at the girls drifting by. Brewer, Towery, Mohr, Snow, Tanner, Kelly! Old comrades, I doubt if you would wish to see it now.

From here the three of us drifted toward the football stadium. We found an unlocked entrance. It sat 35,000 in my time, with a turf of authentic grass. They played only daylight ball then. Here I saw, on a sweltering 100-degree September afternoon of 1952, a Notre Dame team roar on the field for the pre-game drills in T-shirts and shorts, and a Longhorn fan yelled: "Next time they'll come out naked!" I witnessed too the first black football player ever to perform here, a second-string halfback named Duke Washington, for the lowly Washington State Cougars, break free on a seventy-yard touchdown in 1954, and the entire student section rose spontaneously and applauded. I was standing at the finish line of the 1955 Texas Relays with my notepad when Wes Santee of Kansas University missed the first American four-minute mile by half a second. I still have a black spot on my knee from tripping in the cinders during the 400-meters of an intramural track meet of 1956. Just as with the Mexican restaurant, the stadium had the same name but fell short of being the same place. A prodigious second tier rose so high and abruptly among the lights that one could barely see it from the Astroturf.

A catharsis was at hand. Directly across the street from the football stadium had been the most lovely and harmonious baseball field in the United States, the most unusual baseball diamond I have to this day ever known. It was called Clark Field, and it had been carved out of the earth from the limestone all around it. Its roofed grandstand and bleachers had a patina of time, and its entire surroundings were touched with an unhurried grace that behooved the best and most complex of all American games. I loved this field, and it came to represent for me the most enduring spot on the whole campus of the University of Texas. Indeed, to me it became the best place in all this frenetic, pulsating state. Its grounds were always impeccably groomed, its grass a dark green, its outfield fences a tawny brown, and there was the inexorable flow of history behind the matchless locale. The magnificent Longhorn teams had played for decades under Uncle Billy Disch and Bibb Falk, who were the most efficacious college baseball coaches in America. Babe Ruth had performed here, when the major league teams coming north out of spring training would play the Texas Longhorns, and Lou Gehrig, we were reminded, was the only man to hit a home run over the fence in deepest center field. A grove of live oaks, perfect for picnics, where we would bring our girls before the games, led to the main entrance under the grandstand. Was there a finer place in God's creation to spend a placid afternoon in the sunshine with one's favorite coed and one's best pals from Breckrenridge Hall, watching the Longhorns in their burnt-orange and white embarrass the loathsome Texas Aggies?

There was a reason, it must be said, why center field fence of

Clark Field was so far away from home plate. Almost all of deep center field, from left center to right center, consisted of a superb limestone slope, quite sizable and in places dangerously precipitous, with a lawn at the final level crest above, and beyond this the outfield fence itself, bedecked with the American flag on the flagpole. This area was widely recognized through the Southwest as Billy Goat Hill, and it was legendary at the University of Texas. *Billy Goat Hill!* We knew it with abiding affection and respect, for it was the perfect condiment to this most distinctive of baseball stadiums. For generations Billy Goat Hill had been the especial domain of a succession of notable all-American Longhorn center fielders. It was their own suzerainty, and they knew every inch of its inclines and crevices. Each center fielder in his turn inherited the long hidden paths and footholds carved with such arduous care in the limestone by their forebears, who educated the newcomers on how to retrieve the enemy's flies and drives. Each new Longhorn center fielder would make his own secret steps and paths and improve the old ones; the torch of Billy Goat Hill thus passed from one era to the next, for the Hill was of the inheritance.

As a fledgling (and soon-to-be-failed) center fielder, I remember as if time has stood still the knowledgeable scrambles up and down the Hill by the distinguished all-American center fielder of the 1950's, Travis Eckert, as he moved across the pathways to pull in a seemingly impossible fly, or a clothesline drive that seemed destined for a double against the stone. The most memorable defensive play I ever saw by any outfielder ever was in the Texas-SMU game of 1954, when Travis Eckert stumbled twice up Billy Goat Hill, then rolled ahead and snared in his gloved hand a mammoth line drive while lying prone on the level ground near the flagpole; and this was in my memory an act of God, and one of the finest things I ever saw. To the opposition center fielders from Baylor or Rice or SMU or A&M, Billy Goat Hill was an anathema. Sometimes they would try to climb it with their hands, or they would trip on an outcropping and tumble to the grass far below. I once saw a center fielder from TCU kick Billy Goat Hill with both feet in exasperation after he had fallen off it chasing a high fly which became a treacherous, ricocheting triple.

One afternoon after practice, Travis Eckert took me out to Billy

Goat Hill to instruct me in its secrets. H carried with him a hoe, a shovel, and a bucket, for he was working on new footholds. For half an hour he showed me how to play the Hill, pointing out the ingenious landmarks of his predecessors who has once ruled it; we walked its paths for a long time as Eckert instructed me in how to judge a fly and then speed up its paths by instinct. The sun began to fade beyond the football stadium. We moved back a few yards and looked up at the intricate Hill in the shadows of the Texas twilight. "Damn!" Eckert said, "I love this old Hill."

Now David and the Mississippi Chairman and I had reached the northernmost exit of the football stadium. As we walked out, I found myself holding my breath in anticipation. Please, God, make Clark Field be there!

It was an idle supplication. As I gazed across the way, I saw that the site of that honorable spot has been taken over by more brand-new buildings. There was not the slightest trace of what I had once known. My wail of anguish—or was it the starkest of four-letter expletives?—caused my companions to pause in curiosity. How could they possibly have comprehended my melancholia? I started across the street to roam among these modern intruders, to seek something that may have remained, some small yet undying memento. But there were too many ghosts here. I could not go through with it.

We continued our journey now, following a new mall toward the center of the campus again. Here even the tallest trees seemed recent transplants. A quarter of a mile or so beyond this unexpected walkway, a cherished structure loomed into view. It was the old Journalism Building, where I had labored for four years on *The Daily Texan*, ending in my senior year as its editor-in-chief, working myself to exhaustion with my four or five thousand words a day, seldom sleeping, never going to class, drinking interminable coffee in a well-appointed office just beyond these windows before me now, and almost getting expelled from school for the fruits of these efforts. We entered the building, which seemed to be a kind of computer center. My old office and the splendid newsroom had been transformed into a set of crowded cubbyholes. I supposed most of the journalism professors with whom we fought and played who once roamed these corridors we long since dead. Downstairs, the composing room, which had bustled so with energy and intrigue, was dark and abandoned.

Across the way we detoured to the new Communications Center, an immense structure built around a courtyard. I ventured into *The Daily Texan* quarters. Everything was bright and gleaming. Students were at work among the banks of computer terminals. I looked up at a large wall. There, lined in a row, were the individual photographs of all the editors since the paper's inception. I sought my contemporaries: Ann Chambers, '52, '53; Bob Kenny, '53, '54; Shirley Strum, '54, '55, and a version of someone who may have been myself, '55, '56. Beyond my own likeness, the row continued —twenty-five more—so that this wall itself was a testimony to one's passing days.

Later we reached the older sections of the campus. Without warning I would stumble upon some quiet corner which had not changed at all—the little park of live oaks behind the Hogg Auditorium, cul-de-sacs and breezeways and dog-leg paths that greeted me with a calming reassurance. Here, on this bench by the grooved steps, on a lovely spring afternoon, I had told a beautiful girl I loved her. A little farther on, near this mossy terrace the future University Chanceller Harry Ransom, had advised me I should apply for a Rhodes scholarship. Under these very trees, one long-ago midnight, I had composed my "thirty" column for *The Daily Texan*. In this shady courtyard, I had retreated one day to read the words of Jefferson on freedom of expression. Beneath these inplacable mustangs, as part of some forgotten rite. I had been thrown into the waters of the fountain. At the base of this statue I had sat one morning with the baseball players as they readied their cheat notes for an examination, one of them writing a chemical formula in ink on his ankle. Adjacent to this pleasant lane, in the old Experimental Science Building, I was introduced to Byron, Shelly, and Keats by Dr. Sackton to the heady smell of chemicals wafting down the lengthy halls, and his Romantics brought that incomparable spring of my eighteenth year alive for me, and I would emerge into the dappled sunshine under the oak trees, oblivious to everyone around me, reading from the textbook to myself:

> *When old age shall this generation waste,*
> *Thou shalt remain, in midst of other woe*
> *Than ours, a friend to man, to-whom though say'st*
> *"Beauty is truth, truth beauty,—that is all*
> *Ye know on earth, and all ye need to know."*

"What the hell are you mumblin'?" one of the baseball boys, who had been walking behind me eavesdropping, asked.

"I'm practicing my baseball play-by-play," I said.

Perhaps over the sweep of the years, and even in the unsettling odyssey into the past on this particular day, I must have forgotten my profound affection and love for this place. For a moment I felt rather guilty. Yet amidst these pleasing rediscoveries of its unchanging aspects, the awareness of this emotion gratified me immeasurably, as if this comprehension of deep affection were part of an old debt repaid, a gesture of continuity, an affirmation of the heart. I knew too in that moment that this campus with its glittering new appurtenances, its symbols of enormous wealth and power, was beautiful to the young who now inhabited it, just as in its more serene times it had been beautiful to my own generation

On my last night there, I knew I must pay my deferences to Scholz' Beer Garten. It stands alone now on a boulevard of parking lots and government high-rises, and it is a monument in its own measure. Here, in the back garden under the trees, the students and professors and politicians mingled over the big pitchers of Lone Star, and they do so to this day. This was our Oxford Union, our parliament, our training ground, and it is as gently shabby and unprepossessing as it always was. Sitting at the favorite table of our group from those times, I drank some beers to the lost voices.

The Chairman of the Appropriations Committee and I were heading on back to Mississippi that night. Perhaps it was the beer, but as my son David drove us through the campus toward our motel, I suggested one last stop, for a premonition had been mounting in me that I might never see the University of Texas again. We drove down San Jacinto and turned at the football stadium. The night was still and dark. A storm was rising from the Gulf as I got out of the car alone to wander the land where Clark Field had been.

At first, for the dozenth time that day, I could not find my bearings. The grounds had been landscaped for the new buildings—which were a Fine Arts complex—and there were no tangible landmarks for me. Yet I knew right field had been about here somewhere, for the fence had nearly paralleled the road beyond. Once Paul Mohr, the gigantic first baseman, had hit a home run approximately here in a close game on an intentional walk to drive in the winning runs, and after the game he had kept muttering, N.G.N. G. "What does N.G.N.G. mean." I had asked him. H replied: "It means, no guts, no glory."

I walked around a stone terrace to one of the new structures. The infield must have started here, and the pitcher's mound was about there, where the starting pitcher for the next day's game of twenty-five ago had performed the act of love one midnight on a waitress while the rest of us hid under the bleachers watching. Home plate would have been three or four dozen feet from where I now stood. I walked in that direction. Some primal wisp of memory told me the main grandstand had occupied this spot. With that knowledge, I began moving in a direct line outward until I reached a building and moved in a broad circle around it, continuing my straight line on the other side. The ground here rose slightly, and the street was thirty yards or so beyond this perceptible slope.

Something there in that instant flickered in the corner of my eye, some hovering ghost of recognition. I turned to look.

There it was, a little shred of Billy Goat Hill! It was no more than fifteen or twenty feet long, and tapered to the right several yards, but I knew I was not mistaken. I was as sure as I was of the pounding of my heart that this was it. The remnant of the Hill sloped farther upward. There was the trace of a worn path in the stone. I stood silently in the groove and gazed downward, and in the somber night with the new edifices all around, I could sense I was standing in deep center field, and the contours of the destroyed outfield and the ruined diamond of those distant days reappeared as an apparition in my mind's eye, and if I were very quiet I could conjure the roar of the crowds down the concourse of time, and the dim figures of base runners, and the echo of bat on ball sending a line drive toward the precinct where I stood.

I bent down and touched the limestone with my hands. I paid my final solitary homage to Billy Goat Hill. Then I stood up and left it behind me. It would be a long way to Mississippi, just as it always had been.